"An essential read for anyone involved experience and Christian reflection, K.... .... uncovers the foundational importance of the biblical metaphor of stewardship, develops the contribution of earlier writers on the subject, from Peter Block to Scott Rodin, and applies his findings to the work of nonprofit organizations. On the way he provides case studies of steward leadership in practice, examines the relationship between steward and servant leadership models, and clarifies the roles of board, executive and staff members. Overall, a major contribution."

Robert Banks, Centre for the History of Christian Thought & Experience, Macquarie University, Sydney

"This astute historical sketch of the steward from antiquity positions modern readers to grasp the gravity of biblical passages with the steward in view. I especially appreciated the use of ancient quotes, theological principles, contrasting charts and call-out boxes that illustrated key points. In a time when too many Christians are acting like owners, Kent Wilson does more than map a model of the steward leader for readers—he shows us how to recalibrate the compass of our spiritual lives and steward leadership toward faithfulness to our master and Lord, Jesus Christ. Well done!"

Gary G. Hoag, Generosity Monk, press author and international liaison, ECFA

"Kent Wilson is the right person to address the concept of stewardship. Kent is a practitioner! As the head of a family foundation, a leader in the nonprofit world and an international contributor to the nonprofit enterprise, Kent speaks with 'battle smoke' on every concept! I have watched Kent practice what he presents for over twenty years. That's why I'm ordering a copy for every member of the TWR International Leadership Team."

Lauren Libby, international president and CEO, TWR International

"Dr. Kent Wilson presents rich historical and biblical context for why steward leadership is essential in order for nonprofit ministries to thrive. He's done the research and supports his case beautifully with compelling stories of steward leaders who have embraced these principles in how they live and lead. Discover everything you need to alter your thinking and transform your heart as a leader."

Tami Heim, president and CEO, Christian Leadership Alliance

"We are indebted to Kent for this thorough presentation of the uniqueness of the steward leader for nonprofit organizations. His historical survey, biblical foundation and the chapters on the nonprofit board as steward leaders and the nonprofit staff as stewards are especially welcome additions to the field of steward leader studies."

R. Scott Rodin, author of *The Steward Leader*

"When God interrupted my life as a church pastor and called me to found and lead a nonprofit organization ten years ago, I really could have used this book. Rather than borrowing spiritual concepts to buttress popular leadership theory, Kent Wilson mines Scripture and uncovers a fresh perspective on leadership—the leader as steward. This is the basic primer every Christian executive and pastor needs to read, digest, and read again!"

Mike Johnson, founder and president, Ascending Leaders

"Kent Wilson provides a fresh look at steward leadership through the eyes of an experienced nonprofit CEO and the lens of a biblical worldview. *Steward Leadership in the Nonprofit Organization* is a thoughtful developmental guide for any leader."

Al Lopus, president and cofounder, Best Christian Workplaces Institute

STEWARD
LEADERSHIP
IN THE NONPROFIT
ORGANIZATION

KENT R. WILSON

An imprint of InterVarsity Press
Downers Grove, Illinois

InterVarsity Press
P.O. Box 1400, Downers Grove, IL 60515-1426
ivpress.com
email@ivpress.com

InterVarsity Press® is the book-publishing division of InterVarsity Christian Fellowship/USA®, a movement of students and faculty active on campus at hundreds of universities, colleges and schools of nursing in the United States of America, and a member movement of the International Fellowship of Evangelical Students. For information about local and regional activities, visit intervarsity.org.

All Scripture quotations, unless otherwise indicated, are taken from THE HOLY BIBLE, NEW INTERNATIONAL VERSION®, NIV® Copyright © 1973, 1978, 1984, 2011 by Biblica, Inc.™ Used by permission. All rights reserved worldwide.

While any stories in this book are true, some names and identifying information may have been changed to protect the privacy of individuals.

Cover design: Cindy Kiple
Interior design: Beth McGill
Images: VasjaKoman/iStockphoto

ISBN 978-0-8308-4467-8 (print)
ISBN 978-0-8308-9340-9 (digital)

Printed in the United States of America ∞

Library of Congress Cataloging-in-Publication Data
Names: Wilson, Kent R. (Leadership Specialist), author.
Title: Steward leadership in the nonprofit organization / Kent R. Wilson.
Description: Downers Grove : InterVarsity Press, 2016. | Includes
  bibliographical references and indexes.
Identifiers: LCCN 2016011842 (print) | LCCN 2016017715 (ebook) | ISBN
  9780830844678 (pbk. : alk. paper) | ISBN 9780830893409 (eBook)
Subjects: LCSH: Church trustees. | Church management. | Christian leadership.
Classification: LCC BV705 .W55 2016 (print) | LCC BV705 (ebook) | DDC
  254--dc23
LC record available at https://lccn.loc.gov/2016011842

| P | 23 | 22 | 21 | 20 | 19 | 18 | 17 | 16 | 15 | 14 | 13 | 12 | 11 | 10 | 9 | 8 | 7 | 6 | 5 | 4 | 3 | 2 | 1 |

| Y | 35 | 34 | 33 | 32 | 31 | 30 | 29 | 28 | 27 | 26 | 25 | 24 | 23 | 22 | 21 | 20 | 19 | 18 | 17 | 16 |

To Debbie, my wife and partner of forty-two years.

By consistently being true to who God made you to be

you have enabled me to flourish as

he intended me to be.

Contents

Introduction

I have never enjoyed reading long introductions and tend to skip them if they go on and on, so I'll be brief. In fact, all I really want to share with you is the vision that drove me to devote decades to researching and writing on steward leadership, especially to writing this book.

I began my professional working life as an electrical engineer but spent the last thirty years of my working life in the nonprofit world. I've worked for a children's camp, a church, a foundation and a nonprofit Christian publishing company, almost all eventually in the capacity of executive director. I also serve on the board of directors of numerous nonprofit organizations (NPOs), mostly in the role of chairman.

My first exposure to the nonprofit world came through my local Bible church. There a young elder, Alex Strauch, encouraged me to embrace my leadership gifts, and under his mentorship I began preaching occasionally starting at age sixteen. I taught Bible studies almost weekly in high school and started serving as deacon while in college. Working in the church taught me how church leadership is unique compared with other nonprofit organizations and how even the young can be given chances to lead, influence and learn.

In my college years I worked every summer at a children's camp as program director. There I was mentored by the director, Paul Sapp (now deceased), who pointedly taught me about servanthood, accountability, delegation and influence over power.

When I was in my mid-twenties my grandfather approached me one day and asked if I would be willing to take over leadership of the Wilson Family

Foundation, an organization he had started in the 1950s to support publishing of Christian books in third-world countries. I was shocked by his
offer at my young age, but he too said he recognized leadership in me. We
engaged in many conversations about vision, mission, impact for Christ and
the spread of the gospel worldwide. In some ways he was a negative example
for me; his approach to leadership was as a business owner who emphasized
power and authority over influence. But his early vision and obedience to
Christ in creating the foundation continues to have its influence to this day,
some sixty-five years later.

After college I worked as an electrical engineer for a number of years.
I never viewed engineering as a diversion from what some mistakenly call
"full-time ministry" (we are all called as believers to full-time ministry
wherever we are). As an engineer I saw many examples of leadership, both
good and bad, and was given opportunities of my own to lead ethically
and to learn how to lead through influence when one does not have
formal authority.

Since my youth I felt that God would someday lead me into professional
ministry, and so I went to seminary in the evenings for several years. After
graduation God made it clear that now was the time to join the pastoral staff
of my church, so I left engineering behind and became an associate pastor
and teaching elder. Church leadership was a refining process of learning
about team leadership and spiritual leadership. But it was also when I experienced the dark side of leadership, when I allowed my passion for the
church to overshadow my growing family and marriage, causing me to
become a one-sided leader who excelled at ministry and failed at life. I will
never forget the day one of the elders confronted me over breakfast (thank
you, Doyle Roth) and said, "Kent, you can either have the work of the church
or you can have your family, but the way you are living your life right now,
you can't have both. You have to choose." I chose my family and resigned,
feeling as though I had failed as a leader after all those years of learning.

After floundering for months not knowing what to do, God was gracious
and opened an opportunity to join the staff at NavPress Publishing, the
publishing arm of the Navigators. I was hired to do a job in which I had zero
experience (direct marketing), but the publisher saw transferable skills and
potential in this young thirty-year-old. I ended up working at NavPress for

twenty-one years and performed almost every job, finally being asked to lead the organization as executive publisher for the last ten years. At Nav-Press I was a part of a rich mentoring and leader-development environment. NavPress is what we call a "commercial nonprofit" in that it is expected to achieve a spiritual mission as a ministry but at the same time operate like a business with all of the attendant financial and performance disciplines. At NavPress I was able to hone and refine steward leadership when there wasn't a term, literature or defined model for it yet.

Today I work as an executive coach and consultant to business owners and nonprofit executives. I am now the mentor, coach, facilitator and en-courager of other leaders, a leader of leaders. It is the fulfillment of my personal mission to mentor developing leaders to be all God intended them to be.

In spite of such an immersive background in the world of nonprofit or-ganizations and nonprofit leadership, my primary exposure to professional leadership development was through reading general business and lead-ership books, attending occasional leadership seminars and studying the few nonprofit management books available. Like most Christian nonprofit leaders, I found leadership models and resources in the for-profit world, but for the most part those models lacked any biblical basis. I wasn't looking for "*the* biblical model" of leadership (since I believe the Bible focuses on prin-ciples and a leader's character, not on models), but I wanted to learn an approach to leadership that was founded on (instead of supplemented by) biblical principles.

The for-profit leadership models I read did provide a wealth of knowledge about organizational leadership and management, but I became increasingly aware of significant differences in the for-profit and nonprofit worlds. My own experience persuaded me that the nonprofit leader's motivation to produce excellent results had a different basis than that of my for-profit counterparts. The most significant distinction I experienced was an awareness of leading the organization, its people and resources, as a trustee or steward—never as an owner. I also led employees and volunteers who viewed themselves as stewards. I realized that a foundational understanding of one's role as a steward and not an owner was prevalent throughout Scripture but largely absent in the leadership literature of the day.

Through most of my thirty years of nonprofit leadership, I struggled to develop an approach to leadership that conformed to this steward leader image. There were almost no books or seminars that highlighted the stewardship role nonprofit leaders performed. In fact, most of the Christian books on stewardship ignored the application of the steward as leader.

As a result I talked with peers and tried to develop principles of steward leadership on my own. I read dozens of books on general stewardship (discovering that most were written by Christian authors) but found only one at the time that applied stewardship to leadership, and that just barely. Being a Christian and a trained Bible exegete, I sensed that we could find a basis for understanding who the steward was and how stewards led through studying the Old Testament and the parables of Jesus.

I also was influenced both positively and negatively by other nonprofit leaders. Those who led effectively and articulated stewardship concepts in their leadership encouraged me to emulate their style and approach. Those who led as though they owned the organization and ignored the interests of the board and stakeholders increasingly gave me concern that they were violating fundamental principles of nonprofit leadership. At NavPress, an eighteen-million-dollar nonprofit publishing organization at the time, I found fertile ground both for testing my developing concepts of steward leadership and encouraging stewardship behaviors in other employees. The majority of this research and my concepts of steward leadership were developed while serving as executive director of that organization.

The final impetus to formally launch my research came when I read a copy of Peter Block's 1993 milestone book on stewardship and leadership, *Stewardship: Choosing Service Over Self-Interest.* That book thrust the issue of steward leadership to the forefront, but I saw it primarily as a missed opportunity. Block's book never addresses leadership in the nonprofit sector, and it equates steward leadership with the redistribution of power, purpose and wealth. His book does provide useful emphases on servanthood, rethinking the structure of the workplace and democratizing empowerment. But in my view Block misses the essence of stewardship, which is to manage the resources of others to accomplish the desires and goals of the owner of the resources, not their own objectives. That experience set in motion my commitment to contribute to the dialogue through doctoral research, the development of the Steward Leader Institute, and the writing of this book.

I was torn concerning the type of book I wanted to write. On one hand I wanted to write about the steward as leader in every sphere of life, but I know the nonprofit sphere best and hence chose to focus there. I wanted to write a book for all leaders, whether they identified themselves as Christians or not, but my background and life motivation are unquestionably Christian, so I chose to address fellow Christian leaders first. I also wanted to write a book that would be equally used in the classroom and boardroom, but I know that my natural bent is that of a teacher and researcher, so this is a foundational book rather than one a practical application.

So here is my vision: I believe that steward leadership, a recently articulated model of leadership with roots going back thousands of years, offers the greatest hope for the transformation and effectiveness of nonprofit leadership, both for Christian leaders and for the world. If fully embraced, it can change the face of nonprofit leadership forever—for stakeholders, boards of directors, executive directors and staff.

In the following chapters, section one will look at the historical origins of the steward in both classical Greco-Roman and Judeo-Christian cultures. Since the steward is a historical figure that many are unaware of today, I felt it essential to study and explain the role before looking in depth at the manner in which stewards lead and manage others. In section two, we will provide a clear definition of the steward leadership model. Given that steward leadership is a relatively recently articulated approach to leadership, it is necessary to define the model at the outset. The steward model will then be compared to its closest "cousin," the servant leadership model, in order to further elucidate its characteristics and distinctives. Finally, in section three, we will apply steward leadership directly to the various leadership roles in the nonprofit organization: the board, the executive director or CEO, and individual staff members. I could have applied the model to any number of sectors, but the nonprofit sector is a good place to begin.

I think you will come to agree that steward leadership is the best and most historically and biblically based model to help the nonprofit executive become an effective leader of a life-changing organization.

1

The Distinct Challenges of
Nonprofit Organizational Leadership

Walter had lots of business leadership experience. He had worked in engineering for decades in different management and leadership positions, which gave him the confidence in his late forties to fulfill a dream and move to the nonprofit sector. He assumed that his years of business leadership would be a significant contribution to a nonprofit organization in Colorado Springs. Sure, the pay scale wasn't even close to what he was used to, but he had been frugal and was willing to take a paycheck hit in order to replace career ascension with significance. The interview process seemed to point to the organization's desire for the business skills he brought to the table, and as a result he felt affirmed when he was given an executive role. The nonprofit was in obvious need of cleanup and turnaround.

In the first few months Walter focused on getting to know the staff, the board and the constituents. He didn't come with a ten-page plan, just an openness to listen and learn before he gained the emotional right to suggest a strategy. At the time he heard enough comments in the vein of "Finally we have a leader who knows something about business and organizations" that he didn't notice the equally cautious remarks about how "We do things a little differently here than you may be used to in business." As long as he was learning, things were positive. But as soon as Walter started to suggest specific changes in processes, staffing and programming, resistance became more overt. Staff members started commenting that "mission is more important than efficiency" and "numbers don't tell the real story."

Working with the board started feeling like a tug-of-war as members exerted their authority over some of Walter's strategies. Walter had worked with an advisory board in his previous privately held company, but that board was full of industry specialists, whereas his nonprofit governance board was made up of average community members with little or no real leadership experience. He was courageous enough to start giving honest feedback to underperforming staff members but equally perplexed by the resistance of their supervisors and even some board members who spoke about "Mary and Eric's long years of service and sacrifice to the organization."

Walter wasn't trying to turn the organization into a business. He was trying to bring business disciplines into the organization to balance its enthusiasm and passion for mission. "Why can't an organization be as exceptional in its business skills as it is in its social impact?" Walter suggested out loud. He got lip service in return but painfully slow follow-through. As he met more and more donors, he received both affirmation and confused looks as he talked about his vision for the organization. Even the stakeholders he thought would give him unified affirmation seemed to be mixed in their desires and goals for the ministry.

No one who has ever tried to lead an organization would say that leadership is easy. And among the myriad organizations one could lead, the nonprofit organization presents some of the most formidable challenges to the modern leader. In many ways nonprofit organizations share the same qualities and challenges as any other organization, be they corporations, governments, cooperatives, educational groups or other formal organizations. However, they do present some unique and demanding opportunities and challenges. The nonprofit organization is not just a corporation that happens to have donors.

That's why we as leaders of nonprofit organizations need to provide the best leadership we can to organizations and communities that rely so heavily on our services. This book is about learning how to lead your best as a nonprofit board member, executive director or CEO, or staff leader. The fate of our organizations, which are built on public trust, and the fate of our communities, who rely on our services delivered often without charge, rest on excellent leadership.

WHAT MAKES NONPROFIT ORGANIZATIONS DIFFERENT?

Nonprofit organizations (NPOs) have unique characteristics that separate them from for-profit corporations. In an attempt to summarize the greatest difference between the two types of organizations, Peter Drucker focuses on the nonprofit organization's ultimate objective in his foundational book *Managing the Nonprofit Organization*:

> It is not that these institutions are "non-profit," that is, that they are not businesses. It is not that they are "non-governmental." It is that they do something very different from either business or government. . . . The "non-profit" institution neither supplies goods or services nor controls. Its "product" is neither a pair of shoes nor an effective regulation. Its product is a changed human being. The non-profit institutions are human-change agents.[1]

Other authors have also defined the unique characteristics of nonprofit organizations that separate them from businesses. Here are the primary distinguishing characteristics referred to most often.

Preoccupation with nonfinancial outcomes. Most nonprofit organizations do attempt to break even or make a small financial profit to ensure their future viability and growth, but profit is not the primary "bottom line." The for-profit corporation has one overriding objective—to generate profit as measured on an income statement. Although other key indicators are also used, the main criterion of success is always profit. For the nonprofit organization, the overriding objective is less clear, less measurable and less objective—the accomplishment of mission.

Tendency toward providing service. Drucker is on target when he emphasizes the nonprofit organizational role as "human change agent" (most researchers refer to this as a nonprofit's public service role). Although it is true that some nonprofits do create products and compete in the commercial world with for-profit businesses, the vast majority provide a service to the community that is inadequately provided by government or for-profit organizations.

Different tax and legal considerations. Government and society in most countries have chosen to allow nonprofit organizations certain tax concessions, but such concessions usually come with unique legal and reporting requirements.

Private sector non-ownership. Nonprofit organizations are institutionally separate from government, but they are also excluded from any public or private ownership. Nonprofit ownership is implicit or indirect in nature; it is found in stakeholders such as constituents, donors or society in general. Throughout this book the term *stakeholder* will refer to any group or individual that has an implicit claim or share in the organization's outcome by virtue of a direct contribution to or engagement in the organization. This lack of direct ownership presents unique challenges for nonprofit management. The majority of books and articles on nonprofit leadership do not give this challenge justice, and yet, based on my experience, it is one of the foundational realities that a unique model of nonprofit leadership must address in detail.

Self-government. Nonprofits generally are governed by an independent board of non-executive directors who control their own activities separate from government intrusion. As we will see in later chapters, both boards and executive directors can be considered stewards or trustees; the former govern and the latter lead tactically.

Ambiguous accountability. Boards and executive directors both are accountable to the stakeholders of the nonprofit organization. But the definition of who the stakeholders actually are and how the organization's leadership is accountable can be ambiguous. Minimal research has been conducted on the exact nature of this accountability. The challenges created by stakeholder ambiguity are some of the most daunting in nonprofit leadership and need additional research and guidance.

THE CHALLENGES OF DEFINING NONPROFIT LEADERSHIP

Resources created for pastors and leaders of churches, one of the earliest forms of nonprofit organization, date back well over a century. However, leadership studies for nonchurch NPOs only began to surface with any significance after the 1980s. Sources dealing with nonprofit management are far more frequent than those addressing nonprofit leadership, but our focus will primarily be on nonprofit leadership. It is frustrating to observe that when these sources try to define the distinctive challenges of nonprofit leadership (as opposed to for-profit leadership), each study comes up with its own list that only partial overlaps other studies. Since research on nonprofit leadership is relatively new, hopefully there will be more coalescing of the distinctive differences over time.

Dennis Young, who has written a number of articles and books on nonprofit management, begins his 1987 article "Executive Leadership in Nonprofit Organizations" by acknowledging the dearth of studies on the topic.[2] He goes on to highlight the challenges nonprofit leaders face compared with those of business leaders, focusing on external and internal functions. He condenses the nonprofit leader's many external functions in the concept of entrepreneurship, asserting that the entrepreneurial risks undertaken by nonprofit leaders are not that different from those faced by for-profit leaders, with the exception of certain differentiators such as regulatory and stakeholder control and lack of equal access to capital. However, Young sees the nonprofit leader's internal functions—which mostly revolve around personnel management—as highly differentiated from those of the business leader. Nonprofits' personnel-related challenges involve recruitment, public image, quality orientation, missional commitment and resource constraints. Nonprofit leaders are also constrained in their ability to implement compensation systems that reward performance. As one of the earliest studies on nonprofit leadership, Young's findings are a strong starting place for additional studies.

Building on earlier works, Paton and Cornforth also analyze how nonprofit management differs from for-profit management in their article "What's Different About Managing in Voluntary and Non-Profit Organizations?" According to the authors, nonprofit management is different because of

- distinctive purposes (nonprofits pursue social goals that do not easily lend themselves to measurement);

- restrictive resource acquisition (primarily funded by donors who have different expectations than customers);

- diverse stakeholders and governance (there is a much wider variety of stakeholders, which changes the nature of governance); and

- distinctive culture (nonprofits have more participatory forms of decision making and are value driven).[3]

In an article titled "Executive Leadership," Herman and Heimovics find that leaders of nonprofit organizations face special challenges when they are expected to integrate mission, resource acquisition and strategy. According to the authors, in spite of the CEO's subordination to the board of directors, the CEO is still expected to exercise "executive or psychological centrality." They describe six board-centered leadership skills that characterize effective nonprofit CEOs: facilitating interaction, showing respect and consideration, envisioning change, providing useful information, maintaining board structure and promoting board accomplishments. One characteristic the authors particularly single out is usefulness in understanding the political frame, or thinking and acting in politically effective ways.[4] Herman and Heimovics's research provides a supportive focus on the CEO-board relationship—one that is crucial for effective CEO performance. But their research misses a considerable aspect of that relationship: the trustee role that both CEO and board perform, which implies that additional board-centered leadership skills are needed.

One of the most significant and detailed treatments of the nonprofit leader is Nanus and Dobbs's 1999 book *Leaders Who Make a Difference*. These authors propose that the primary purpose of nonprofit leadership is to focus laser-like attention throughout the organization on the greater good the organization is capable of providing, and then to marshal energy and resources to make that greater good happen. The greater good is produced by maximizing the social goods the organization can produce for society and the people it serves. Social goods include organizational capital (assets that embody the potential to produce social goods) and social energy (the energy that is generated when a nonprofit organization marshals common action for the common good). Nonprofit success, and to a degree its leader's success, can be measured by studying the output and impact of all three: social goods, organizational capital and social energy. Nanus and Dobbs also evaluate the distinctive roles nonprofit leaders embody to build an organization—that of visionary, strategist and change agent—and three roles that strengthen relationships—politician, campaigner and coach.[5] Given that this book presents one of the more detailed treatments of nonprofit leadership, and that it recognizes the service role in attempting to produce the greater good, it is unfortunate that the authors do not include in their list the essential role of stewardship (which was proposed ten years earlier by other writers).

In the article "A Leadership Model for Nonprofit Projects" (found in the book *Improving Leadership in Nonprofit Organizations*), Victor Sohmen focuses on developing a distinctive nonprofit leadership model for nonprofit projects. Nonprofit projects are flexible, temporary group entities composed of volunteers and idealistic participants who are tasked to produce a project with specific tasks and timelines. Sohmen applies three existing leadership models to nonprofit project groups—transformational leadership, visionary leadership and servant leadership—and concludes that all taken individually are deficient. He suggests that nonprofit projects require a multidimensional model that combines the best of all three leadership models triangulated into one flexible model that is strategic and value oriented.[6] Sohmen concludes by listing ten essential factors of this model of nonprofit project leadership, which leaves the reader with the impression of a model that is so "multidimensional" it is impractical.

The following list summarizes the most common themes surrounding the unique characteristics of nonprofit leadership from those who have written on the subject. Nonprofit leadership is distinctive from for-profit leadership because of

- constraints on nonprofit entrepreneurial activity (such as regulatory and stakeholder control and lack of equal access to capital);

- constraints on leaders' ability to recruit personnel and to implement compensation systems that reward performance;

- a distinctive social mission, purposes and goals (which do not easily lend themselves to measurement);

- restrictions on resource acquisition (which is primarily driven by donors who have different expectations than customers);

- diverse stakeholders (which changes the nature of governance and accountability);

- a distinctive culture (more participatory forms of decision making and a value-driven culture);

- the need for leadership to express values important to the organization;

- the balance of CEO centrality and submission with regard to the board;

- usefulness in thinking and acting in politically effective ways; and

- focused attention on the greater good the organization is capable of providing, and marshaling energy and resources to make that greater good happen.

THE INADEQUACIES OF EXISTING LEADERSHIP MODELS

The above list of nonprofit leadership distinctives highlights the unique challenges in leading nonprofit organizations and the need for a specific model of nonprofit organizational leadership. But no single model exists. In my experience leading multiple nonprofit organizations, both as executive director and as a board member, there are additional challenges that remain inadequately defined in existing leadership models:

- the motivation nonprofit leaders have for leading and managing well when personal benefit is disconnected from performance;

- the challenge of responsibly managing resources that one has no direct ownership of or financial stake in;

- the stewardship role that both executive and non-executive directors play (and the interaction between both parties as a result);

- the nonprofit leader's relationship with God and stakeholders;

- the role of God and stakeholders in determining the goals and objectives of the organization (and how the leader balances varying input); and

- the nonprofit leader's accountability to God and the stakeholders of the organization.

There is no doubt that nonprofit leadership is difficult given the sobering statistics emerging concerning most nonprofit leaders' limited tenure and the future of nonprofit leadership. A study of more than two thousand U.S. nonprofit executive directors called "Daring to Lead 2006" by Bell, Moyers and Wolfred raises important questions about the precarious future of executive nonprofit leadership. Their findings are summarized in five statements:

- A majority of nonprofit executives plan to leave their jobs—but not the nonprofit sector—within five years.

- Boards of directors and funders contribute to executive burnout.

- Executives believe they make significant financial sacrifices to lead nonprofits.

- Concerned with organizational sustainability, executives seek new skills and strategies.

- Bench strength, diversity and competitive compensation are critical factors in finding future leaders.[7]

In a 2001 precursor to the same study, nearly two-thirds of nonprofit executive leaders were found to be in the executive role for the first time, and fifty-one percent of nonprofit executives had been in their role for four years or less.[8] The authors also found that three-quarters of nonprofit executives planned on leaving their jobs within the next five years and affirmed that statistic five years later in a follow-up study. Multiple studies of the nonprofit sector have also raised disturbing trends in the turnover rate for nonprofit executives and rising rates in leadership transition due to aging. These studies provide an important context for any model of nonprofit leadership that hopes to be effective in addressing the unique challenges nonprofit leaders face.

In my review of nonprofit leadership books and articles, I discovered that the most common leadership models used by authors to address the distinct challenges of nonprofit leadership are transformational leadership, servant leadership, visionary leadership and various forms of spiritual leadership (in faith-based nonprofits). In a survey of leaders of Christian-based nonprofit organizations that I conducted in 2010, I found that executive directors followed a variety of approaches to leadership, many of them simultaneously: eighty-two percent claimed to follow the servant leadership model, seventy-four percent the team leadership approach, fifty-one percent the transformational leadership model, forty-one percent steward leadership and twenty-three percent the situational leadership model. Many of the other traditional models of leadership (democratic, transactional, contingency theory and other more specialized forms of spiritual leadership) came in with less than single digits as a percentage.

In the introduction I described how I tried multiple approaches to nonprofit leadership, only to find most of them lacking. I knew there was no "perfect" model out there that fit every leader, organization or occasion, but there had to be an approach that addressed both the biblical principles of leadership and the unique needs of the nonprofit organization. Servant leadership had both biblical roots and appropriately fit the mindset of the nonprofit world, but it failed to address many nuances of nonprofit work. Team leadership was an attractive challenge, but stakeholders typically held the top leader accountable, not the team. And none of the leadership models wrestled with a significant issue that I kept coming back to, which was my

TRYING TO FIND A NONPROFIT LEADERSHIP APPROACH THAT WORKS

The nonprofit leader is a unique animal. In my search for a theory of leadership that speaks directly to the idiosyncrasies of this type of leadership, I often met with frustration and discouragement. Secular leadership models needed too much adaptation for use in a Christian context. Christian approaches seemed on one hand to be nothing more than a Christianized version of these secular theories or, on the other, not really models at all but simplistic lists such as "12 things to do to be a great leader."

A common problem was that they all started with what a leader does instead of who a leader needs to be. That's the defining mark, the core competency and striking uniqueness of a leader called by God to serve in his kingdom. Even servant leadership misses the mark here. The focus still is on how a servant approach to leadership produces results rather than what it means to cultivate the heart of a true servant. For that reason I find the steward leadership model to be revolutionary. It begins with the changed heart of a man or woman called by God to be a faithful steward and then applies that transformation to his or her role as a leader.

In this way the steward leader is profoundly biblical. The approach is founded on our call to be disciples and focused on kingdom outcomes. It has been a great joy and relief to set aside the need to translate secular leadership theories or try to check the boxes on the lists of practices associated with successful leaders. The steward leader calls us into deeper intimacy with Christ, a more profound level of obedience, absolute freedom and real joy in leadership. For that reason it is truly transformational in the best sense of the word.

—SCOTT R.

sense of the need for accountability as a non-owner to God and the stakeholders of the organization.

The fact that nonprofit executive leaders apply a wide variety of leadership approaches to their role can be seen in a positive light when we consider that these leaders are trying to be as contextual as possible in their leadership, responding to the circumstances at hand with the best applicable model. However, given the fact that most traditional leadership models are derived from research and studies in the for-profit sector, this varied approach may well have a negative side. Since the late 1980s it has been demonstrated repeatedly that the challenges of nonprofit leadership are distinct from for-profit leadership. Given this fact, is nonprofit leaders' shotgun approach an indication of their desperate need for a distinct leadership model? Is there an approach that addresses not some but all of the challenges presented to non-profit leaders? I think the time is right for a model of nonprofit leadership derived from the unique role nonprofit leaders perform and the distinct challenges that make the nonprofit organization different from a business.

Any effective model of nonprofit leadership would need to address most or all of the primary characteristics that distinguish a nonprofit organization from a business. It would also have to give direction and solutions to the distinctive challenges nonprofit leaders face. It would need to particularly address the nonprofit leadership challenges that current leadership models do not adequately consider:

- the motivation of nonprofit leaders to lead well (a steward's altruism);

- resource management of non-owner leaders (a steward's role);

- the stewardship roles associated with various levels of nonprofit leadership (a steward's scope);

- the relationship of the nonprofit leader with God and stakeholders (a steward's focus);

- the challenge of identifying and balancing the goals and objectives of God and stakeholders (a steward's challenge); and

- the leader's accountability to God and stakeholders.

A New Model of Nonprofit Leadership

This book proposes a new nonprofit leadership model derived from the biblical, historical and cultural foundations of the nonprofit sector. As we study the historical role of the classical and biblical steward, we will find a foundation for what many nonprofit leaders recognize as their primary identity: they are stewards of resources that belong to others. They lead organizations, missions and resources that they do not own. The steward leadership model is not new (it was proposed back in the 1980s), but it is new with respect to a concise and detailed application to nonprofit leadership.

SECTION ONE

The **HISTORICAL ORIGINS** *of the* **STEWARD**

The steward leadership model is one of the few models that begins with a historical figure. Understand who the steward was in history and you will understand this approach to leadership much more deeply. In section one we'll take an unprecedented look at the historical origins of the steward in both Greco-Roman and Judeo-Christian cultures. We will define and characterize the role of the steward so that we can understand the unique aspects of how he managed and led within social and business organizations.

2

The Historical Steward of Classical Greco-Roman Culture

Nonprofit organizations have roots that can be traced as far back as ancient Egypt and Rome with the establishment of voluntary religious and educational associations in these societies. But the strongest surge in charitable voluntary not-for-profit organizations occurred within the last two hundred years in England and colonial America. Because of the inadequacies of government intervention (what some call "government failure") and the absence of civil organization, private citizens were forced to come together to address social, educational, cultural and human issues within their communities and work together to find solutions. Even when governments developed a presence within a particular community, citizens were afraid of the bureaucracy associated with government control and often sought solutions through voluntary associations. These voluntary or charitable organizations were soon recognized by government and given social, organizational and tax considerations in exchange for constraints on "ownership," governance and financial distributions.

When governments started officially sanctioning nonprofit organizations, they reached back to the ancient concepts of stewardship, trusteeship and fiducia to delineate the public trust and common ownership that was temporarily being placed in the hands of the organization's leaders. To protect the public interest and help accomplish the common good, nonprofit organizations were structured so that they belonged to the communities they served and could not be owned by any individual. The leaders of such organizations were temporarily granted fiduciary responsibility (also called "trusteeship") over the organization because they held it "in trust" for the community and could never benefit as owners. In overseeing the assets and activities of the organization, the trustees were required to carry out the fiduciary responsibilities of "duty of care, loyalty and obedience." They were stewards in every sense of the word: people who managed resources they did not own on behalf of others. So to best understand the stewardship role of modern nonprofit leaders, we need to look at the classical steward of ancient society.

Today in our culture we may hear an occasional reference to a union shop steward, airline steward, wine steward or ship's steward, but beyond these obscure references to certain types of service personnel, the role of steward is largely unknown. To understand how to lead a nonprofit organization with the mindset of a steward, it is helpful for us to go back to a time when stewards were well-known members of society, when the details of the steward's role and responsibilities were first documented. Variously referred to as the bailiff, manager, house manager, overseer or steward in classical societies, the steward was given the responsibility of managing the resources of the master on his behalf or in his absence.

Stewards played a significant role in Chinese, Egyptian, Hebrew, Greek, Roman, Jewish and medieval societies. Up until the fourth century BC, they were mentioned only briefly in funerary inscriptions and business documents, and no description of the steward's role existed in writing. However, starting around 360 BC, agricultural manuals began to surface from a few classical Greek and Roman writers—Xenophon in Greece; Marcus Cato, Marcus Varro and Lucius Columella in the Roman Republic and Empire—explaining the specific roles and responsibilities of the steward. Because of cultural and educational restrictions, nothing was written by stewards themselves of their role, but only by their masters. Historians acknowledge that these documents most likely contain some bias as to the master's expectations of his steward's role, but they are the only detailed record researchers have to work with and still serve as a valuable window into everyday classical society and stewardship.

THE STEWARD IN GRECO-ROMAN SOCIETY

Ancient wars produced an abundant supply of slaves. Numerous Greek and Roman victories supplied such a large flow of labor that the nature of work and leisure was changed for everyone from the upper classes down to the common soldier. Slavery was a horribly abusive and demeaning practice, but with this growth of slave labor also came the growth of industry, estates and large urban farms (or *latifundia* in the Roman Republic), which required a large pool of labor and organized local management. As Greek and Roman citizens increasingly viewed common work as demeaning for both philosophical and social reasons, they gradually gave over management of the slave workforce to specially trained and authorized managers or stewards chosen from the slave pool. A slave would often be identified at a young age for his management potential and trained over time in all aspects of work to someday assume the role of steward.

According to Arnold Jones, slaves and stewards were more common in urban industry than on the farm: "Only the home farm where the landlord resided was normally cultivated by slaves. Slaves were more commonly employed in industry. . . . As Xenophon puts it, 'Those who can, buy slaves so as to have fellow workers.' That is, craftsmen who could afford it bought slaves and trained them as assistants, hoping ultimately to retire and live in their declining years on the proceeds of their work."[1] Because of this, elaborate laws evolved (particularly in the Roman Empire) to define owners' legal responsibility for their slaves' commercial transactions, and many laws surfaced to govern the actions of slaves who were vested with authority to act on their masters' behalf.

Greek and Latin words for steward. Various Greek and Latin words were used in ancient times to describe the role of the classical manager or steward. The most common Greek word for steward was *oikonomos*, a compound word that John Reumann in 1957 etymologically analyzed as coming from the noun *oikos*, meaning "house"—or, by extension, "household"—and the verb *nemō*, meaning "to deal out, distribute, or dispense."[2] *Oikonomos* also came to mean by derivation "to rule" or "to manage." Early in the classical period the term referred to one who managed a household, but later it came to be used of a broad range of household administrators, estate stewards, business managers, subordinate state officials and financial officers as well as holders of public office. The word had extensive associations with industry, politics and religion as well as with the common household. Brown, Driver and Briggs add this:

Oikonomos (from Aeschylus on) was used of people, and has a more concrete meaning. It denotes the house-steward, and then by extension the managers of individual departments within the household, e.g., the porter, the estate manager, the head cook, the accountant, all domestic officials who were mostly recruited from among the slaves.[3]

The second most common word associated with the role of the steward in Greek is *epitropos*, which designates a person to whose care something has been committed.[4] The word is used in reference to the guardian of a minor, a steward, a trustee or an administrator, along with political officials such as a procurator or governor. The term is frequently used for a guardian of a minor orphan but not always with regard to inheritance. The *epitropos* was appointed by the father or, for an orphan, by the court so that he or she could act in place of parents in all matters related to the child's welfare and life.

Other Greek words associated with the steward include *tamias* (one who cares and distributes, dispenser, steward, housekeeper) and *phrontistēs* (one who takes care, a house-steward).

Although Latin occupational titles were numerous, *villicus* was the most common word used for the farm overseer or steward. It was also used for servants employed in public service and managers of businesses. The Latin word is generally translated into English as "steward," "overseer" or "bailiff." Other Latin titles used for managers or overseers include *procurator* (the person who manages a business), *dispensator* (an administrator or treasurer), *negotiator* (the slave manager of a master's business), *institor* (a business manager) and *actor* (an agent or business manager). John Crook reveals the breadth of the steward's responsibilities by describing the various roles typically associated with each Latin name:

> At the highest level was the steward, *servus actor* or *dispensator*, who managed the accounts and carried out the financial transactions of the wealthy families and their estates. . . . Free men were willing to pass into slavery to secure this coveted position, and the *dispensator* could expect to receive freedom on properly rendering account to his deceased master's heir. He might be in charge of estates abroad, entirely on his own. . . . He might, as *actor publicus*, be city treasurer of a municipality. Then, on a rather lower level of standing, there was the *vilicus* or *bailiff:* managing a particular agricultural property, in

charge of all the labour, slave and free. . . . Then again, the slave might manage enterprises outside the family range altogether, such as taverns and shops; apparently even "children" (adolescents, one supposes) ran such places— often, according to Gaius. And, going back to businesses, we hear of a slave (who decamped) managing a mixed affair that included money-lending, pawn broking, and letting depository space to grain merchants; and Ulpian envisages the possibility (though the way he puts it suggests it is a marginal one) of a slave being a full-scale banker.[5]

General duties of the steward. Slaves were broadly classified into two groups: overseers and workers. Overseers, or stewards, were generally slaves but some were freedmen (a former slave released from slavery), and in rare instances may have been free men (born citizens) who sold themselves into slavery to become overseers. Slaves and freedmen were chosen as steward-managers because their masters "preferred to use in positions of trust men whose characters they knew, and on whose obedience they could rely; slaves could be chastised if they disobeyed instructions, and freedmen had formed the habit of executing their master's orders."[6] It is important to note that most stewards who were slaves remained slaves for life. Although some received their manumission, rarely was their freedom granted by virtue of their role as stewards. In later chapters we will see how important the characteristic of servanthood is to anyone who leads as a steward.

Greek and Roman stewards managed the farm, estate or business finances and resources on behalf of the master or owner. According to Keith Bradley, stewards could be employed as managers in a wide range of enterprises:

> In everyday commercial life—that is in activities such as shopkeeping, trading and banking—slaves were particularly noticeable, operating as their owners' managers and agents with a great degree of latitude and independence, a pattern clearly shown by a section of the Digest (14.3) that deals with the contractual liability of those who appointed agents to undertake business for them. The agent, who could be free or slave, a man or a woman, was called an *institor* and was appointed "to buy or sell in a shop or in some other place or even without any place being specified" (Digest 14.3.18). Any number of enterprises could thus be in the hands of slaves—managing a farm, buying houses, cattle or slaves, shop keeping and inn keeping, banking and money lending, trading and contracting of every kind.[7]

The steward's management role was considered by many as prestigious. Socrates, for instance, likens the steward's role in estate management to a branch of knowledge (*epistēmēs*) similar to medicine, smithing and carpentry.[8] In a 1994 translation of and commentary on the works of Xenophon, a Greek writer, soldier and mercenary who studied under Socrates, Sarah Pomeroy comments on the status he attributed to *oikonomikos* (or estate management): "The prestige awarded to the management of the *oikos* [household] in classical Greece may come as a surprise to the modern reader who may be familiar with the activities of the Greeks in the public sphere and who may also despise 'housework.' However, the *oikos* was fundamental to the welfare of human beings and their cities."[9] Pomeroy quotes Socrates, speaking in another book by Xenophon on moral philosophy (*Memorabilia*), when he calls the role of *oikonomia* a *mathema*—a learning or science. Both Plato and Socrates also refer to *oikonomia* as an *epistēmēs*, or field of knowledge.[10]

On larger urban farms it appears that more than one steward could be present. According to the ancient Roman historian Varro, "If you cultivate less than 240 iugera of olives you cannot get along with less than one overseer, nor if you cultivate twice as large a place or more will you have to keep two or three overseers."[11] Varro does not provide detail about how multiple stewards on one farm related to one another, but stewards were elsewhere known to have understewards (see the next chapter on stewards of the Old Testament). Stewards were also allowed under certain conditions to own and administer property (*peculium*), which could have involved the ownership of other slaves (*servus vicarious*) and possibly other understewards.

Based on these descriptions of classical stewards and what we learn from the Judeo-Christian steward in the next chapter, I propose this definition: *A steward is someone who manages resources belonging to another person in order to achieve the owner's objectives.*

The social status of the steward. Classical stewards who were slaves could not escape the hard realities of their social position. They lacked most if not all the fundamental freedoms of a citizen and were under the complete ownership of another person. They had no individuality, no legal personality apart from that of their owner, no *patria* (fatherland) and, in the eyes of the law, no male parent.[12] In both Greek and Roman societies, attitudes about slaves' innate capacities changed over time. In the Homeric world, slaves were viewed simply as captured foreigners held by force who possessed all the characteristics and virtues inherent in human beings but with none of the privileges or rights of a citizen. The slave was a piece of property but not a beast. However, after Aristotle proposed that there were natural differences in slaves' innate moral and intellectual capacities, slaves were increasingly viewed as subhuman—somewhere between animals and humans.[13]

Discussing classical slavery and the steward, classics professor William Thalmann adds his perspective on this contradiction:

> One of the things that has always struck me about Xenophon and the Roman writers . . . is their suspicion of slaves and whether you could really trust them as slaves. How much of a free hand do you give them? How often do you audit their accounts? What do you do when you find them not performing well? And in Xenophon's case, how do you train them so that you can ensure their loyalty?
>
> The answer is: You do it the way you would train a horse because the slave is like an animal. The *villicus* focuses the dilemma of the slave owner. The master's got this person under his power whom he has to think of as a kind of thing but who is actually a person with a certain amount of thought and autonomy, and has to be induced to do what his master wants him to do. The whole relationship is always a very tense one. If slaves are inferior, then you can't trust them, and yet you have to trust them.[14]

However, the social status of stewards, and the ensuing attitudes of their masters and the general public, were not all negative. Funerary inscriptions for stewards abound in praise of their loyalty, longevity, faithfulness and appropriate exercise of authority. Stewards experienced a form of occupational hierarchy in which they were considered superior to other domestic slaves, and their prestige increased with the size of the estate or farm they managed or the social standing of their owner. City stewards (*urbani*) were considered more prestigious than country stewards (*rustica*). Assigning slaves to managerial positions produced interesting anomalies at times: stewards often served as bank managers, could rise to highly respected positions within local government as treasurers, and on large rural farms often collected rents and supervised the activities of tenant-farmers who were freedmen or free men.[15]

THE RESPONSIBILITIES OF THE GRECO-ROMAN STEWARD

The roles and responsibilities of the classical steward are laid out in surprising detail by several Greek and Roman writers, but only in the context of the *oikonomos* or *villicus* of the rural farm. Xenophon wrote his Socratic dialogue *Oeconomicus* around 360 BC. It is one of the earliest Greek works on economics and principally focuses on household management, agriculture, relationships between men and women, slavery, and rural life.

Three Latin writers stand out for writing works that aid our understanding of the classical steward on the Roman farm. The second-century statesman, soldier and author Marcus Porcius Cato (234–149 BC) wrote *De Agri Cultura* around 160 BC on running the *latifundia*, or rural farm, including in it a collection of husbandry and management rules. Cato's manual assumes a farm run and staffed by slaves, and his harsh suggestions for dealing with sick or unproductive slaves are striking in their severity. Marcus Terentius Varro (116–27 BC), a Roman scholar and writer, was called "the most learned of the Romans" by Cicero and St. Augustine of Hippo. Although he wrote more than four hundred works, only two survive, one of which is his advice on agriculture and beekeeping. Finally, Lucius Junius Moderatus Columella took up farming after a career in the army and serving as tribune in Syria. His twelve-volume *De Re Rustica* (written around AD 60–65) has been completely preserved and forms the most important source on classical Roman agriculture and urban slavery.

All four classical writers produced manuals on agriculture for the benefit of fellow landowners. In their manuals they describe the responsibilities of the steward and, in some cases, the corresponding responsibilities of the steward's wife. Although biased toward the interests of the master, these descriptions are the most detailed records researchers have concerning the classical steward's responsibilities. Table 1 summarizes the characteristics and responsibilities of the classical steward based on these works.

Any assemblage of classical steward characteristics and responsibilities from the writings of Xenophon, Cato, Varro and Columella is an approximation at best since these authors did not prescriptively define a steward's role. However, we can extract the general traits and tasks of a steward based on repeated themes in these documents.

Table 1. General characteristics and responsibilities of Greco-Roman stewards

Personal Characteristics	Preparation for Management
• Medium age	• Taught from childhood
• Robust	• Trained in all aspects of farming
• Not physically attractive	• Trained for management
• Vigorous	
Personal Virtues	**Absence of Personal Vices**
• Diligent	• Not intimate with household members
• Early riser and last to go to bed	• Not a drunkard
• Energetic	• Not lazy
• A frugal eater	• Avoids sexual indulgence
• Does things in moderation	• Not superstitious
• Always learning	• Not a gadabout
• Faithful	• Does not expect special treatment
	• Does not show favoritism
Relation to Master	**Use of Resources**
• Fidelity and attachment	• Keeps tools in good repair
• Knows what his master knows	• Knows the cost of proper tools is cheaper than idle workers
• Follows his master's instructions	• Uses the same resources as the workers
• Insures that the master's orders are carried out	• Knows where he can quickly obtain more resources if needed
• Does not use his master's money to engage in personal business	• Gives additional resources as rewards to others who do well
• Does not think himself wiser than his master	• Does not scrimp on resources (such as seed)
• Frequently reviews the accounts with the master	
• Does not give excuses for work left undone	
• Does not lend out his master's property	
• Loyal	
Management Skills	**Management Skills (continued)**
• Able to teach others	• Protects workers from wrongdoing to avoid punishing
• Demonstrates by example how a job is to be done	• Humors good workers
• Assigns tasks appropriately	• Disciplines in proportion to the wrong
• Personally leads workers to the job site	• Keeps workers busy
• Encourages the workers	• Produces workers who are themselves enthusiastic, eager and persevering
• Rewards good workers	• Knows how to command others
• Is always available	• Does not do other people's work for them
• Expects a full day's work from everyone	• Controls who comes and goes on the estate
• Plans ahead	
Relation to Subordinates	
• Cares for the health of workers	
• Provides adequate food and clothing	
• Does not expect subordinates to serve him	
• Not too cruel or lenient	

Personal characteristics. Columella is the only one of the four classical writers who focuses on the steward's personal characteristics, and he does so with intentional specificity. The ideal steward must be of medium age in order to have the right balance of skill and vigor, "for slaves despise a novice as much as they despise an old man, since the former has not yet learned the operations of agriculture and the latter cannot any longer carry them out, and his youth makes the novice careless while his age makes the old man slow."[16] The steward should also be of sound health, married to a woman who can help him in his management duties, and be neither physically attractive nor ugly.

Personal virtues and vices. The virtues of the steward are very important to the classical writers, and all four go into detail about the qualities that are important for proper exercise of the role:

- *Hard working.* The steward should be able to perform all of the duties of the slaves while avoiding doing the work for them. "He must take pains to know how to carry out every agricultural operation, and must do so frequently, but never to the extent of tiring himself out."[17]

- *Always growing in knowledge and experience.* "This above all else is to be required of him—that he shall not think that he knows what he does not know, and that he shall always be eager to learn what he is ignorant of; for not only is it very helpful to do a thing skillfully, but even more so is it hurtful to have done it incorrectly."[18] We don't know whether the expectation of growth was extended to the normal working slave, who was no doubt provided less opportunity to learn. But stewards were encouraged to recognize what they needed to learn and were given the freedom to develop needed skills.

- *Moderate in personal indulgences.* The steward was not to be addicted to wine, sleeping in, socializing, sexual indulgence, gluttony or superstition.

- *Morally and sexually self-controlled.* Xenophon and Columella both warned stewards not to be sexually active with other slaves. "He should also have an aversion to sexual indulgence; for, if he gives himself up to it, he will not be able to think of anything else than the object of his affection."[19] To help the Roman steward avoid the temptation of sexual exploitation or harassing the other slaves, he was granted the benefit of a nonlegal wife (*vilica*) to satisfy his sexual needs—a benefit that was withheld from most ordinary slaves.[20]

Stewards were also to be responsible, diligent, frugal and skilled in all of the jobs.

Preparation for service. Development of leaders was not just the purview of the Roman aristocracy; estate owners were also encouraged to proactively develop the stewards of tomorrow. They did this by identifying potential candidates at an early age, then teaching and testing them to develop their skills. Stewards were selected and trained for management by the master himself or by existing estate stewards.[21] They were put through a testing process to see if they could learn farming and management and would demonstrate fidelity to the master.[22] Their training involved exposure to almost every job on the farm so they could not only do the job but also teach others how to do it: "Whoever is destined for this business must be very learned in it and very robust, that he may both teach those under his orders and himself adequately carry out the instructions which he gives."[23] Xenophon includes an extended dialogue between Socrates and Ischomachus in which the latter explains how he teaches future stewards through praise, recognition with special clothing and rewards, and punishment when necessary.[24]

Relationship with the master. The relationship of the steward to the master was one of the most important domestic relationships in the Greco-Roman family. Consequently, all four of the writers mention different aspects of the master-steward relationship. Stewards were to:

- *Be respectful.* "He must not think that he is wiser than his master."[25]

- *Be obedient to the master.* The steward was supposed to listen intently to what the master said and follow his orders.

- *Be aware of the master's desires and intentions.* Classical estate owners were aware of the inherent risks associated with nonvested management and addressed the situation in part through a master's extensive training and mentorship: "I train him up myself; for he who stands in my place in my absence and acts as a deputy in my activities, ought to know what I know."[26]

- *Protect the master's resources.* "Cato's rules for the *vilicus* or manager are partly an attempt to ensure that he has no relationships with, or obligations to, any gods or humans except through the owner. The post was one of great responsibility. A bad manager could do lasting damage to the owner's property and ruin his business and his relations with neighbors."[27]

- *Be accountable for his actions and results.* Cato mentions a detailed process of accountability the master should go through when first arriving on the farm and meeting with the steward. The process involved reviewing the workers' efficiency, the condition of the resources and the state of the accounts, culminating in a realistic assessment of the steward's successes and failures in managing the resources.[28] "He should frequently go through the accounts with his master."[29]

- *Accept the master's lifestyle.* The steward was expected to take on the gods of his master, oversee the religious activities of the farm and even accept his master's friends as his own.

- *Stay within the objectives set by the master.* "He should not employ his master's money in purchasing cattle or anything else which is bought or sold; for doing this diverts him from his duties as a bailiff [steward] and makes him a trader rather than a farmer and makes it impossible to balance accounts with his master."[30]

Relationship with subordinates. Stewards were unavoidably reminded every day that they were slaves in service to their masters. But with their privileged position on the estate, stewards could have found it easy to assume that other slaves existed to serve their needs. Not so fast, says Columella: "He should not make use of his fellow-slaves for any service to himself."[31] Columella goes into great detail to define his expectations of how the steward and his wife should treat the other slaves. The steward was to look out for the health and protection of the working slaves and along with his wife make sure all were provided with adequate clothing and food appropriate to the season and work conditions.[32] The steward was not allowed sexual intimacy with any member of the extended household except his wife: "This same overseer should be warned not to become intimate with a member of the household."[33] When the workday was done, the steward was to exercise the care and compassion of a shepherd: "And when twilight has come on, he should leave no one behind but should walk in rear of them, like a good shepherd, who suffers no member of the flock to be left in the field. Then, when he has come indoors, let him act like that careful herdsman and not immediately hide himself in his house but exercise the utmost care for every one of them."[34] The steward's management of the workers was to be a balance of discipline that was not too severe or too lenient,[35] with some humor and forbearance.[36]

Use of resources. For the classical steward on the rural Roman farm, resources were as practical as iron hoes and slave labor. But not all resources had the same implicit value. The classical manager was expected to know that the unavailability of cheaper resources (such as tools) could cause the waste of more valuable resources (such as slave labor): "He should rather often examine the iron tools. These he should always provide in duplicate, and, having repaired them from time to time, he should keep his eye upon them, so that, if any of them have been damaged in the course of work, it may not be necessary to borrow from a neighbor; for it costs more than the price of these things if you have to call off the slaves from their work."[37] The steward was also to maintain a resource reserve by always knowing several neighbors whom he could borrow tools from when needed.[38]

The steward's wife was responsible to maintain the food and clothing stores and ensure that both lasted throughout the year.[39] Seed corn was neither to be squandered nor scrimped so that it was used properly to ensure a good crop. It was the steward's responsibility to guard the property from intrusion and from outsiders changing the borders. The steward was not allowed to lend money or resources to others without the master's permission. All in all, the steward was responsible to manage all of the master's resources, whether things or people, with foresight, efficient application and long-term sustainability in mind.

Management skills. The four classical writers spent most of their attention on instructions for how the steward was to manage the farm and its workers. Many of the following instructions are still a part of today's modern management philosophy. Stewards were to:

- *Teach from personal experience and example.* The steward was to lead by example. "From time to time, as if to aid one whose strength is failing, he should take his iron tool from him for a while and do his work for him and tell him that it ought to be carried out in the vigorous manner in which he himself has done it."[40]

- *Motivate through encouragement, humor and reward.* Surprisingly, stewards were instructed to encourage, humor, reward and honor workers who responded well and showed promise. "He must reward good work so that the others have an incentive to work well too."[41]

- *Discipline and correct appropriately.* A steward was instructed "not to deal either too cruelly or too leniently with those set under him. He should always cherish the good and diligent and spare those who are not as good as they ought to be, and use such moderation that they may rather respect his strictness than hate his cruelty."[42]

- *Produce good work in others.* "The man in charge—whether he is a foreman [*epitropos*] or a supervisor [*ephestēkōs*]—who can produce workers who are enthusiastic, eager for work, and persevering; these are the ones who manage to prosper and to make their surplus a large one."[43]

- *Wisely allocate people resources to the right tasks.* "The most important thing in this kind of superintendence is to know and estimate what duties and what tasks should be enjoined on each person. . . . The nature therefore of each operation must be taken into consideration; for some tasks require strength only, such as the moving and carrying of heavy loads, [while] others require a combination of strength and skill."[44]

- *Exercise authority and control at all times.* The steward was delegated authority by the master and was expected to learn how to manage and lead "like a general" with constantly changing strategies and deployment of resources.[45] The steward had complete control of who came and went from the estate: "No one shall leave the farm without the direction of the overseer."[46]

THE CLASSICAL STEWARD AS PRECURSOR OF MODERN MANAGERS

The modern manager will no doubt recognize many elements of contemporary management philosophy among the responsibilities of the classical steward. Here are nine responsibilities that illustrate the level of sophistication in managerial science that existed even as far back as the fourth century BC.

Always learning. Drawing on their extensive research, Bennis and Nanus describe effective leaders as those who are "enthusiastic learners, open to new experiences, seeking new challenges, and treating mistakes as opportunities for self-improvement."[47] Such attitudes, and the unexpected opportunity to be a lifelong learner, were also offered to the steward-slave. The steward enjoyed a startlingly open environment that encouraged honesty concerning one's level of ignorance, an eagerness to learn, and progress toward the development of useful skills.

Trained for management. Estate owners were encouraged to choose potential candidates at an early age, teach them and develop their skills to be future managers. One might assume the master-slave relationship to be predominantly servile and subservient. But the connection between the classical master and steward must have been distinctive in order for it to be characterized by an emotional bond of "fidelity and attachment," traits that have largely disappeared from modern management in favor of independence and self-realization.

Not sexually indulgent. Sexual misconduct in the workplace is the subject of management books today, and such warnings were also articulated thousands of years ago. The explicitly clear warnings against sexual relationships between steward and coworker range from unwanted intimacy to sexual pursuit: "Let him particularly avoid intimacy with members of the household and even much more with strangers. . . . Further, he should also have an aversion to sexual indulgence; for, if he gives himself up to it, he will not be able to think of anything else than the object of his affection; for his mind being effused by vices of this kind thinks that there is no reward more agreeable than the gratification of his lust and no punishment more heavy than the frustration of his desire."[48]

In possession of the owner's knowledge. A unique relationship exists between owner (principal) and manager (agent) in which the latter agrees to act in the interests of the former through delegated authority. According to agency theory, agents tend toward self-interest and need to be directed through control structures and incentives in order to achieve the interests of the owner. An alternative theory called stewardship theory (articulated starting in 1990) holds that there is no conflict of interest between manager and owner because of the altruistic and intrinsic motivations of the steward-manager to act in the interest of the owner. Classical owners of estates and farms with stewards approached the situation in part through training and mentoring. In a conversation between Socrates and Ischomachus concerning how a farm owner trains his steward, the advice is given: "If someone is going to be capable of taking charge in my place when I'm away, what else does he need to know other than what I do? If I am capable of supervising the various types of work, surely I can teach someone else what I myself know."[49]

Aware of the cost of tools versus labor. Former PepsiCo president Andrall Pearson states that of the many tasks that managers should know how to perform, one of the most fundamental is the ability to marshal resources. Leadership consultant Bob Biehl supports this claim in his definition of leadership: "Leadership is knowing what to do next, knowing why it is important, and knowing how to bring appropriate resources to bear on the need at hand."[50] Resources for the modern manager range from people to equipment, time and money. For the classical steward on the rural Roman farm, resources were seed corn, hoes and slaves. But not all resources have the same implicit value. If the right tools were not available, valuable labor could be wasted.

Not expectant of service from those below. A steward was forbidden from using his privileged position to demand servitude from the other slaves. Today servant leadership is in vogue, articulated by notable voices such as Greenleaf, Blanchard, Block and De Pree. According to Peter Block, the primary task of the steward, and the work of stewardship, involves choosing service over self-interest.[51] Expanding on that concept, Larry Spears adds, "Stewardship, like servant-leadership, assumes first and foremost a commitment to serving the needs of others. It also emphasizes the use of openness and persuasion, rather than control. Stewardship and servant-leadership are closely aligned ideas that reflect the growing trend within many institutions."[52]

A good example. "For indeed nothing can be taught or learned correctly without an example, and it is better that a bailiff should be the master, not the pupil, of his labourers. Cato, a model of old-time morals, speaking of the head of a family, said: 'Things go ill with the master when his bailiff has to teach him.'"[53] According to Richard Ayres, leading by example is an unquestioned management and leadership principle today: "Leadership, then, is the act of setting the right example, serving as a role model, having actions that speak louder than words, standing up for what you think is the 'right' thing, showing the way, holding to the purpose and espousing the positive beliefs."[54]

Willing to reward. Today entire books are available on the various nuances of effective motivation. For instance, the *Manager's Desk Reference* encourages effective supervisors to "motivate by giving regular and specific performance feedback, by coaching employees to improve their performance, by encouraging employee growth and development, and by rewarding good performance."[55] Although threat of punishment would seem to be the most common incentive within a slave society, one finds surprising references where stewards are encouraged to give honor and reward to deserving slaves: "He should celebrate festal days by bestowing largesse on the strongest and most frugal among them [the slaves], sometimes even admitting them to his own table and showing himself willing also to confer other honours upon them."[56]

Able to produce workers who are themselves motivated. Xenophon encouraged stewards to produce workers who were enthusiastic, eager for work and persevering. Today we call this "empowerment." "Long before empowerment was written into the popular vocabulary, exemplary leaders understood how important it was that their constituents felt strong, capable, and efficacious. Constituents who feel weak, incompetent, and insignificant consistently underperform."[57] The challenge of producing workers who were "enthusiastic, eager for work, and persevering" must have been difficult indeed within the slave culture, but it was not unheard of.

By now I hope it is clear that we can identify many of the behaviors and responsibilities of the ancient steward-slave in the neglected descriptions of classical Greek and Roman writers. In these four classical writers—Xenophon, Columella, Varro and Cato—we find surprising antecedents to both for-profit and nonprofit management today. This chapter has touched in detail on some of these managerial traits, and the next will add to our understanding by exegeting the historical steward in the Judeo-Christian writings and stories of the Bible, providing a wealth of historical material on the steward and stewardship.

3

The Historical Steward
of the Bible

In this chapter we will focus on defining a biblical typology of the historical steward that is germane to the nonprofit leader, whether faith-based or not. Several important purposes drive this stage of our study. First, the biblical passages provide a theological and historical platform for the steward's role and characteristics, along with a benchmark with which to compare one's understanding of the contemporary steward. Also, the biblical texts concerning the steward are some of the most detailed descriptions we have of historical stewardship, so to ignore them would be to ignore God's principles on leadership. The biblical history reveals the behaviors and expectations of the steward from a great diversity of cultures and across a wide span of time. In the parables of Jesus in the New Testament alone are some of the most fascinating and informative applications of the steward's role to religious and business leadership.

Thus we now move from the classical steward, whose time spanned the fourth century BC to the first century AD, to the biblical steward, who spans an even broader history: from as far back as the second millennium BC in the Old Testament to the first century AD in the Pauline writings of the New Testament. This study of the biblical records will be primarily historical and exegetical (as opposed to theological) and will focus on the characteristics and behaviors of the steward in the Old Testament era, the parables of Jesus and the letters of Paul.

THE STEWARD IN THE OLD TESTAMENT

We'll begin our study of the steward and stewardship in the Old Testament by identifying and analyzing the common Hebrew words for steward used in the Masoretic text, the Hebrew text of the Jewish Bible.[1] We will then examine the primary scriptural passages in the Old Testament that elaborate the behaviors and expectations of the steward, focusing on those that contain information beyond simple use of the title. This section will conclude with a summary of the main Old Testament concepts behind stewardship and the steward's role.

Hebrew words for steward. The Hebrew phrase that is most commonly used in the Hebrew Bible for those in the position of steward is *'al habbayit.* *'Al* is a Hebrew preposition that denotes elevation or preeminence and is variously translated "above" or "over." *Bayit* is the most common Hebrew word for "house," but by metonymy the word can also denote what is in the house, or "household," which includes household affairs, persons and property. Thus the phrase came to mean "he who is over the household" and is generally applied to those in official positions over the household of an important official. Notable examples of *'al habbayit* stewards in the Old Testament are Joseph as the steward over Pharoah's palace (Gen 39:4; 41:40), an anonymous steward over Joseph's house (Gen 43:16, 19; 44:1, 4), and Ahishar as steward of King Solomon's palace (1 Kings 4:6). The position had a wide range of responsibilities and official statuses, beginning with private household management and extending to second-in-command to the pharaoh or king. David Gersch singles out Eliakim, steward of King Hezekiah's palace, as an example:

> Eliakim (Isa. 22:19-23; 2 Kings 18:18) is not merely manager of the royal household, but takes on an office, distinct in itself within the court, of governing the well-being of the people of the land. Since *'al habbayit* or *ho oikonomos* cared for the household of the king, the welfare of which was conjoined to the welfare of the nation, the position held by this person could naturally have been transformed into the first official of the state below the king.[2]

Another Hebrew word that gives insight into the background of the steward is *na'ar,* which generally is translated "boy" or "youth" but also is used to refer to servants, personal attendants and household servants.

Several clear uses make it apparent that the word occasionally referred to official stewards of entire families and kings. In 2 Samuel 9:9-10 and 19:17, Ziba is called the *naʿar* of the house of King Saul and is obviously a well-to-do person—with fifteen sons and twenty slaves of his own—who officially negotiates for Saul's family. In 2 Kings 19:6 the prophet Isaiah refers to the *naʿarim* of the king of Assyria, which included an individual given the official title of chief commander in an earlier passage (2 Kings 19:4).

Other less frequently used Hebrew words that correspond with the role of steward are *rab bayit* ("chief of the house" in Esther 1:8) and *pecha* ("lord of the district" in Esther 8:9). There are also occasions when the generic word for "servant," *ʿebed*, is used to describe a steward (Gen 24:1-67; 41:12), but only context can differentiate the generic servant from the official steward-servant. Therefore according to David Gersch, all four of the most common Hebrew words that refer to the steward share two aspects in common:

> First, the terms can refer merely to a major-domo or to a government officer, whose office apparently grew out of the common major-domo position. Secondly, the two offices share in a generic character: each position involves the administration of another's property and each receives its own authority from a higher authority. The name and well-being of this higher authority is closely associated with and determined by the work of the delegated officer.[3]

Primary Old Testament passages on the steward and stewardship. We now turn our attention to the primary Old Testament passages that contain references to the role and behavior of the steward or to stewardship. Although some of the passages will not contain the specific Hebrew words previously reviewed, the passages are important nonetheless for establishing the biblical understanding of the steward or stewardship. In the following review of key Old Testament passages, we will observe these principles that help us understand the ancient Judeo view of stewards and stewardship:

- God is the owner of all creation.
- People are God's representatives on earth.
- The steward has both dependent and independent authority.
- Joseph as the prototypical steward.
- The danger of acting like an owner.

God is the owner of all creation (Ps 24:1; Deut 10:14).

The earth is the LORD's, and everything in it,
    the world, and all who live in it. (Ps 24:1)

To the LORD your God belong the heavens, even the highest heavens, the earth
and everything in it. (Deut 10:14)

Based on our definition of stewardship (stewardship is the management
of resources belonging to another in order to achieve the owner's objectives), to understand stewardship we must begin by establishing proper
ownership of the resources. The Genesis account of creation begins the
biblical record with the view that God is the creator of all substance: "In
the beginning God created the heavens and the earth" (Gen 1:1). And because God is the Creator, he is also the sovereign owner of all creation as
well. This establishes a biblical economic foundation regarding ownership.
In the Old Testament, humanity is given temporary ownership of land by
divine gift, but perpetual human ownership was forbidden and regulated
through various economic laws. For instance, regulations for the Jubilee
Year—where land and property temporarily sold were restored to their
original owners every fifty years—are defined in Leviticus 25:23-28 to
prevent permanent ownership and to confirm that "the land must not be
sold permanently, because the land is mine [God's] and you reside in my
land as foreigners and strangers" (Lev 25:23).

Unfortunately, it is easy for humans to assume that if we have been given
resources by another to use and develop, and we have grown those resources due to our own abilities and skills, we should also be given some
aspect of ownership. But when God is the owner and giver of the resource,
Deuteronomy clearly cautions against such presumption: "You may say to
yourself, 'My power and the strength of my hands have produced this
wealth for me.' But remember the LORD your God, for it is he who gives you
the ability to produce wealth" (Deut 8:17-18). God not only provides all
resources for mankind's use; he also provides the ability to develop and
multiply those resources. According to Deuteronomy 8, the failure of stewardship is forgetfulness, pride, failure to obey the divine giver, and presumption—all symptoms that the steward has forgotten his or her role and
assumed the role of an owner. Therefore, the behaviors of the steward in

this passage are thankfulness (praise) for being entrusted with resources to use, constant awareness (remember) and respect for the existence and rights of the true owner, obedience to the master's desires and commands, and humility of spirit.

People are God's representatives on earth (Gen 1:26-27).

> Then God said, "Let us make man in our image, in our likeness, and let them rule over the fish of the sea and the birds of the air, over the livestock, over all the earth, and over all the creatures that move along the ground." So God created man in his own image, in the image of God he created him; male and female he created them. (Gen 1:26-27)

The image of God in humanity, or the *imago Dei*, has been extensively interpreted by theologians and relates directly to people as stewards of God. In the ancient Near East, a king would sometimes erect an image of himself in a territory as a symbol of his sovereignty. In a similar vein, humans can be seen as God's representatives on earth since they bear God's image. There was also the belief among some Near Eastern peoples that their king was the image of their god. The king was like a deity, standing in the deity's place as his representative ruler on earth. The source of this concept can be seen in the words of Genesis 1:26, particularly given the fact that the Genesis statement goes on to correlate the *imago Dei* through humanity's role in ruling over all of creation. As God's creation "in his own image," man functions as God's representative ruler or delegated authority on earth. Therefore, to represent or to "image" God is a fundamental concept undergirding the stewarding role. Humanity stands in the place of, and works on behalf of, the ultimate owner. The *imago Dei* dictates the means by which people steward creation. We are to rule creation as the divine owner would rule it.

Thus, instead of ruling violently or consumptively over creation, people fulfill their stewardship by ruling as the image of God—peaceful and benevolent—according to the pattern set by the divine owner. Even though these passages speak of humanity's delegated stewardship only over nature, we will discover later in this chapter that the same principle of stewarding with care and respect applies equally to other resources, such as people and spiritual truths. Since all things are owned by God, we are to steward each resource as God would, regardless of the type of resource. Earth stewardship is not an option in the Bible's mind, but rather the foundation and starting point for appropriate stewardship.

Having reviewed the Old Testament biblical passages that establish the foundational concepts important to a biblical view of stewardship—God's ownership, humankind as God's steward and the divine gift of abilities—we will now consider Old Testament passages that elaborate on the characteristics and behaviors of the steward.

The steward has both dependent and independent authority (Gen 24).

> Abraham was now old and well advanced in years, and the LORD had blessed him in every way. He said to the chief servant in his household, the one in charge of all that he had, "Put your hand under my thigh. I want you to swear by the LORD, the God of heaven and the God of earth, that you will not get a wife for my son from the daughters of the Canaanites, among whom I am living, but will go to my country and my own relatives and get a wife for my son Isaac." (Gen 24:1-4)

Although the servant of Abraham referred to in this passage is never given the formal title of steward, descriptions within the passage clearly identify him in that functional role. He is called "the chief servant" and "the one in charge of all that he had." This servant is given an unusual task by Abraham—to find a wife for his son Isaac. During this period of time, fathers normally chose the spouse for their children, but in this case Abraham was advanced in years and probably unable to travel. He thus assigns the task to his most trusted servant. In the process of completing this task we see certain characteristics of the steward:

- He is in charge of everything that his master possesses, including people, wealth and things (Gen 24:2, 10, 53-54).

- He is trusted to find an appropriate wife for his master's son (Gen 24:4).

- His freedom to act is limited only by explicit directions from the master (Gen 24:1-9).

- Commitments made to or by the steward are the same as commitments made to or by the master (Gen 24:49).

- He is free to exercise independent judgment in how to best fulfill his obligations (Gen 24:12-14, 56).

An overarching characteristic of the steward exemplified in this passage, and reflected on occasion in the classical Roman steward, is the master's confidence in the steward that involves both dependent and independent authority. Helge Brattgard sees this characteristic extended to all stewards:

> What is remarkable about the biblical idea is the fact that the steward has a unique authority. He is a fully authorized representative, free to deal independently on behalf of his master, at the same time that he is completely dependent upon his master. When his stewardship is over he will have to give an account of how he took care of the calling which, as just noted, involves both dependence and independence.[4]

Joseph as the prototypical steward (Gen 39:1-6; 41:38-41).

> Now Joseph had been taken down to Egypt. Potiphar, an Egyptian who was one of Pharaoh's officials, the captain of the guard, bought him from the Ishmaelites who had taken him there.
>
> The LORD was with Joseph and he prospered, and he lived in the house of his Egyptian master. When his master saw that the LORD was with him and that the LORD gave him success in everything he did, Joseph found favor in his eyes and became his attendant. Potiphar put him in charge of his household, and he entrusted to his care everything he owned. From the time he put him in charge of his household and of all that he owned, the LORD blessed the household of the Egyptian because of Joseph. The blessing of the LORD was on everything Potiphar had, both in the house and in the field. So he left in Joseph's care everything he had; with Joseph in charge, he did not concern himself with anything except the food he ate. (Gen 39:1-6)
>
> So Pharaoh asked them, "Can we find anyone like this man, one in whom is the spirit of God?"
>
> Then Pharaoh said to Joseph, "Since God has made all this known to you, there is no one so discerning and wise as you. You shall be in charge of my palace, and all my people are to submit to your orders. Only with respect to the throne will I be greater than you."
>
> So Pharaoh said to Joseph, "I hereby put you in charge of the whole land of Egypt." (Gen 41:38-41)

Joseph, the youngest of twelve brothers, is sold into slavery at the age of seventeen by his jealous brothers to a traveling band of Ishmaelites

(Gen 37:2). He is then resold to Potiphar, an official of Pharaoh in Egypt. Joseph doesn't sulk in his slavery but uses the occasion to serve Potiphar to the best degree possible, a mark of a diligent steward-in-training. Thus Potiphar elevates him to the position of steward (*'al habbayit*, Gen 39:4) over the entire household and agricultural estate. The fivefold repetition that Joseph is put in charge of "all that he had" (Gen 39:4, 5, 6, 8) emphasizes the comprehensive scope of the steward's authority over all resources, save only the food that Potiphar ate (Gen 39:6) and intimate access to his wife (Gen 39:9).

However, it is on the latter restriction that the entire story turns as Potiphar's wife unsuccessfully attempts to seduce Joseph and then, as a spurned lover, falsely accuses him (Gen 39:7-18). Joseph is immediately thrown into prison with no possibility of defense, illustrating the stark reality that a steward, however high in authority or power, is fundamentally still a slave without rights. A steward may have almost complete authority and scope over all that the master owns, but never total authority or freedom.

Joseph languishes in prison for more than a decade. While there he exhibits the same spirit of service and attentiveness, which soon catches the eye of the prison warden, who places all the prisoners under Joseph's authority (Gen 39:20-23). While in prison, Joseph also befriends Pharaoh's cupbearer—thrown in prison for offending Pharaoh—and reveals the meaning of a dream to him. Years later, after the cupbearer is restored to his original position, Pharaoh has a dream he cannot interpret. The cupbearer remembers Joseph and tells Pharaoh about him. Pharaoh sends for Joseph and is so impressed with his discernment and wisdom (Gen 41:39) that he makes him second in command over the palace (Gen 41:40) and the entire land of Egypt (Gen 41:41). Joseph's authority is once again powerful and limited only by claim to the throne (Gen 41:40). Joseph's official title isn't stated, but it is clear that he functions in a steward leader role.

The study of Joseph in Egypt is complicated due to the fact that, without official title or rank defined in the record, it is hard to distinguish between responsibilities that are a function of steward leadership and those that are a function of his official role. However, a number of distinct characteristics of Joseph's duties surface in this highly detailed account that are informative of the steward leader's role:

- Steward leadership can be expressed at many different levels and circumstances—on the estate, in prison or even at the national level—whenever
  a superior (the principal) trusts an inferior (the agent) with resources and
  responsibilities belonging to the superior.

- Stewardship can involve a wide scope and high level of responsibility,
  including the oversight of all of the resources of the principal—both
  property and people—exclusive of personal resources (for example, the
  master's wife, Gen 39:9) or positional resources (for example, titular authority, Gen 41:40).

- A critical requisite for a master/owner is that he can trust his steward.

- Faithfulness and success as a normal servant/slave can be an important
  prerequisite for elevation to the status of steward.

The danger of acting like an owner (Is 22:15-19).

This is what the Lord, the LORD Almighty, says: "Go, say to this steward, to
Shebna, who is in charge of the palace: What are you doing here and who gave
you permission to cut out a grave for yourself here, hewing your grave on the
height and chiseling your resting place in the rock? Beware, the LORD is about
to take firm hold of you and hurl you away, O you mighty man. He will roll
you up tightly like a ball and throw you into a large country. There you will
die and there your splendid chariots will remain—you disgrace to your master's house! I will depose you from your office, and you will be ousted from
your position." (Is 22:15-19)

Occasionally the biblical record speaks of a steward that has failed in his
official duties, such as in the case of Shebna, steward in charge of the palace
of King Hezekiah. In this story, the prophet Isaiah is sent by God to speak
against Shebna, who was acting more like the master than the steward-slave
he was. Among other things, he was building a sepulcher for himself and
his family (stewards were prohibited from being buried among the social
elite). Later references to Shebna confirm that he was demoted to the lower
position of scribe for his actions (Is 36:3, 11-12; 37:2; 2 Kings 18:37). Helge
Brattgard sees in Shebna's negative example an illustration of several important stewardship principles: "His faithlessness resulted from the fact that
he never discovered life's stewardship principles, viz., God's sovereign
lordship and man's total responsibility on the basis of this. His attitude of

selfishness had not been broken. He lived in the belief that he was to seek his own good as long as possible. Responsibility for others and for the need of giving an account had been lost."[5] Douglas Hall identifies another important principle of stewardship in this passage—a steward needs to always remember that he or she is still a slave or servant and not a master:

> However important the steward may be in the scheme of things, he is neither ultimately authoritative nor irreplaceable. He may indeed be a superior servant . . . but he is still a servant: and if he forgets this and begins to behave as though he were himself unambiguously in charge (i.e., not accountable) he shall be dealt with most severely.[6]

Major stewardship themes in the Old Testament. The previous review of key passages from the Old Testament demonstrates that the steward played a significant role in ancient biblical history. We have seen the themes of ownership, creation stewardship, faithfulness and trust, dependent and independent authority, and the danger of acting like an owner in the biblical record. We will now summarize the major stewardship themes that emerge from these stories (as well as other Old Testament stories that space does not allow full treatment).

Stewards as representatives of the one whose resources they manage. One of the first foundational concepts presented in the Old Testament—alongside establishing God's ownership over creation—is that humanity is created in the image of God, or *imago Dei* (Gen 1:26-27). *Imago Dei* is the theological concept that asserts that human beings are created in some fashion after, with or in God's image and therefore have value and distinction apart from other animal and plant life. Robert Ellis affirms that the image of God in man is foundational to a biblical understanding of stewardship: "To speak of humans as God's representative rulers is to speak of their stewardship."[7] As a biblical theology, *imago Dei* speaks primarily of one's relationship as steward to God, and inferentially of one's relationship as steward to other human beings (for example, nonprofit organizational stakeholders). This aspect of the representational nature of stewards has a number of implications:

- Stewards share certain characteristics with their masters (or the owner of the resources) that allow them to manage the resources as functional representatives.

- Stewards must be in relationship with their masters to appropriately serve as their representative. This relationship exposes the steward to the necessary knowledge, awareness and understanding that allow him or her to "image" or represent the master accurately.

- Ruling and exercising dominion over resources are part and parcel of the steward's role just as they are integral to the master's role.

- The steward exists to be the face, hands and image of the master in the same way that humans were created to be the face, hands and image of God on earth.

Just as biblical stewardship is rooted in the continuous image-bearing of God, it exists as a quality of continuous being more than an action that is performed from time to time. By being the image of God, humanity also bears the identity of a steward. Ben Gill connects continuous image-bearing with stewardship:

> Stewardship is not one remote decision grounded in the past; the essence of life as a steward is a daily answering to the call of God. Stewardship is not the static signing of a pledge card in the annual drive (although this concreteness is not without significance). Stewardship is a responding with my "Yes" to God's constant call that I live life in God's image, as God's steward responding to God's will. This sense of being daily addressed as a steward uplifts life from the banal struggle for existence and places it on a plane of the redemptive.[8]

God's sovereign ownership and humanity's stewardship. From the very first interaction between God and man recorded in the Bible, the foundational principles of God's sovereign ownership over earth, and humanity's role as stewards, are at the forefront. Although an owner has the right to exclusive control and personal use of his or her resources, the Bible clearly indicates that God chose to share control and consumption of his creation by positioning humanity as his trustees, stewards and representatives. God does not share ownership, but he does permit humanity to act as "temporary owners" as long as his divine ownership is always acknowledged.

Richard Taylor elaborates on this tension between divine ownership and human possession:

In the Genesis account, God created the earth and set men and women in it to tend it according to God's will. When this is combined with the idea of the Divine Fatherhood, the earth is seen as being given to people in trust so that they will use its resources to sustain the human family. These ideas suggest that God wants humans to look upon themselves as trustees of their possessions, property, and productive capital, seeking to use them in the light of their understanding of God's purposes.[9]

Another important biblical principle is that all humanity is given stewardship of creation, not just a select few. Therefore, no single person or group of people has the right to view any other person or group as anything less than fellow stewards, equally created in God's image and equally given the responsibility of stewardship.

The master's trust and the steward's authority. Specific examples of stewards in the Old Testament demonstrate the essential authority and trust masters placed in their stewards. The master vested representational authority in his steward that was both wide-ranging and dependent. Stewards were trusted to represent their masters in most personal and business affairs and were able to exercise a limited level of independent judgment and authority. Even at the divine level, God vests authority in humanity to rule and exercise dominion over his creation in accordance with the same care and attention he gave to creating the world. All such authority is rooted in the steward's intimate knowledge of the desires and principles of the master.

The human master's trust in the steward is different. At the human level, trust in the steward's faithfulness is earned slowly as the steward proves himself through successive responsibilities. But God gave humanity stewardship responsibilities regarding his creation as a gift of grace before humans could demonstrate any trustworthiness. Still, God's gift of stewardship is not an eternal entitlement, and at various times in biblical history God rejected humanity's irresponsible stewardship of the earth and judged people groups for violating that stewardship.

The Steward in the Parables of Jesus

A study of the characteristics of the steward in the New Testament spans less than a century of time and contains both didactic stories of stewards (as told by Jesus in the parables) and the Pauline Epistles addressed to the young Christian church. As we will see, both sources offer distinctive presentations of the steward that need to be studied separately and in detail to develop a more comprehensive typology of the biblical steward. An exhaustive review of all pertinent New Testament passages on the steward and stewardship would be a significant scope of work in and of itself (since in the parables alone sixteen of the thirty-eight parables told by Jesus are concerned with stewardship). Therefore we will focus only on the roles and responsibilities of the biblical steward as demonstrated in the primary New Testament parables and Epistles.

We begin with a review of the Greek words for steward to establish a baseline for the historical and cultural context that both genres of the New Testament share in common.

Greek words for steward. The words used in the Greek New Testament for the steward have already been reviewed in the chapter on the classical steward. The most common word is *oikonomos*, a compound word that early in the classical period meant "one who manages a household" but that came to refer to a broad range of household administrators, estate stewards, managers, subordinate state officials, financial officers and any official holders of an office. The word did acquire religious connotations before it was adopted by the biblical writers when it was used of persons who were given responsibilities in connection with non-Christian cultic practices. Among the uses of *oikonomos* in the New Testament, we find three main types:

- a manager of a household or estate, (house) steward, manager (Lk 12:42; 16:1, 3, 8; 1 Cor 4:2; Gal 4:2);

- a public treasurer (Rom 16:23); and

- one who is entrusted with the administration of spiritual matters (1 Cor 4:1; Tit 1:7; 1 Pet 4:10).

The second-most-common word associated with the role of the steward in the New Testament is *epitropos*, which designates a person "to whose care something is committed." It is used of the guardian of a minor, a steward, a trustee, an administrator or a political official such as a procurator or governor.

Exegesis of Jesus' parables on the steward and stewardship. A popular form of narrative instruction used by Jesus is the parable, a short story drawn from the common culture of the day used to illustrate a moral or spiritual lesson.

The parable of the faithful steward (Lk 12:42-48).

"Who then is the faithful and wise manager [*oikonomos*], whom the master puts in charge of his servants to give them their food allowance at the proper time? It will be good for that servant whom the master finds doing so when he returns. I tell you the truth, he will put him in charge of all his possessions. But suppose the servant says to himself, 'My master is taking a long time in coming,' and he then begins to beat the menservants and maidservants and to eat and drink and get drunk. The master of that servant will come on a day when he does not expect him and at an hour he is not aware of. He will cut him to pieces and assign him a place with the unbelievers.

"That servant who knows his master's will and does not get ready or does not do what his master wants will be beaten with many blows. But the one who does not know and does things deserving punishment will be beaten with few blows. From everyone who has been given much, much will be demanded; and from the one who has been entrusted with much, much more will be asked." (Lk 12:42-48)

This is the first parable in the Gospels to mention the *oikonomos*.[10] It gives the reader a clue as to first-century expectations of the duties and attitudes of the steward by illustrating opposing examples of two types. On the one hand, the "faithful and wise" steward begins his responsibilities by dispensing the allocations of food to the other slaves, and because of his reliability he is advanced to take charge of all the master's possessions. In an opposite framing of the story, Jesus presents the same steward taking advantage of his master's absence by indulging a false sense of independence in abusiveness, self-gratification and excessive consumption. This steward can only expect the most severe kind of judgment from his master.

Jesus' conclusion to the parable supplies the reader with further clues as to potential roles and responsibilities of the steward. It is not enough that the steward know the will of his master—he is expected to act on it. His accountability as a steward is in proportion to the amount of responsibility entrusted to him. The steward is to view his responsibilities as a banker would view investments placed in his trust—he must eventually return to the owner more than what was deposited.

Thus, this first parable of stewardship reveals a number of characteristics and responsibilities of the steward:

- The attitude of the steward is such that he recognizes that the resources he oversees are not his own but his master's. He uses them entirely at the will and order of the master—not at his own will or for his own selfish consumption.

- Appropriate character traits of a steward are faithfulness and trustworthiness, qualities that help ensure proper use of resources that are not one's own.

- The steward is to carry out his duties with watchfulness, always ready to be held accountable when the master returns (see the parable in Lk 12:35-40, which develops in more detail this attribute of watchfulness and alertness).

- The master will often reward faithful service with greater responsibility and resources.

- One potential resource entrusted to a steward is the care and oversight of the other people.

- A steward has various relationships that he or she is responsible to manage, which Scott Rodin identifies as

  1. the relationship of the steward to the master or owner of the resources

  2. the relationship of the steward to the resources themselves

  3. the relationship of the steward to the recipients of the resources

  4. the relationship of the steward to himself or herself.[11]

- The greatest abuse a steward can commit is to treat the resources in his charge as though they existed for his personal consumption. If caught in such a state, he is liable for discipline or judgment in proportion to his awareness of his responsibilities.

- Stewards are severely condemned for hypocrisy or a lack of integrity by acting one way in the presence of the master and another in his absence.

A parable of resource management (Lk 13:6-9).

Then [Jesus] told this parable: "A man had a fig tree, planted in his vineyard, and he went to look for fruit on it, but did not find any. So he said to the man who took care of the vineyard, 'For three years now I've been coming to look for fruit on this fig tree and haven't found any. Cut it down! Why should it use up the soil?'

'Sir,' the man replied, 'leave it alone for one more year, and I'll dig around it and fertilize it. If it bears fruit next year, fine! If not, then cut it down.'" (Lk 13:6-9)

In the process of warning a crowd of listeners of the importance of personal repentance (Lk 12:54-59), Jesus is confronted by some in the group who present him with a commonly accepted moral assumption. They suggest that people who suffer disaster must have been greater sinners than others (Lk 13:1-5). To quell this common misconception, Jesus tells this parable about an unfruitful fig tree. Most commentators interpret Jesus' story as a warning to his listeners of their urgent need for repentance and of God's patience to punish, but the parable contains valuable information about the steward as well.

The parable assumes that fruit-bearing plants should eventually bear fruit. Even more so, a fruit tree planted in rich soil that remains unfruitful after a reasonable number of years shouldn't continue to occupy valuable resources (in this case, fertile soil) that could be directed elsewhere. Both the farmer and the vinedresser agree on this. Although the vinedresser is never specifically called a steward, his actions clearly represent stewardship principles and accountability. But what is interesting about Jesus' parable is that the vinedresser—acting in his role as a steward—feels the freedom to suggest a final experiment to help the resource produce fruit by fertilizing it for one more year. The steward was aware of the master's ultimate objective—trees should produce fruit—but had a close enough relationship with the master to suggest an alternative path to that objective.

In my experience, this parable identifies a potential blind spot in many Christian nonprofit leaders. Nonprofit managers sometimes persist in investing in nonproductive activities under the pretext of mission faithfulness ("we are staying faithful to our mission") or limited definitions of accomplishment ("if we can impact just one person for Christ, it's still worth it"). Christian nonprofits often engage in campaigns, projects and activities without ever measuring the results or assessing the effectiveness of the resources invested. By doing so they confuse activity with mission, assuming that as long as they are busy

ONE OF MY HARDEST DECISIONS AS A STEWARD LEADER

A major issue I face as the CEO of a faith-based nonprofit organization is how to determine success of our programs. One of our outreaches is a pregnancy resource center providing pregnancy tests, ultrasounds and options counseling for women and men facing unplanned pregnancies. In trying to measure success, what is the value one assigns to a life? How do you measure how many lives need to be saved for a program to be called successful?

One of our longtime donors was convinced that we needed a mobile pregnancy unit in order to reach clients in their neighborhoods, so he bought a used RV and delivered it to our office. He also recruited a large group of supporters and raised funds for the operation of the unit for the first year. Because it was a used RV and not equipped for running the heater and air conditioner all day, there were logistic issues from the beginning. In addition, we were not seeing the clients we thought we should be seeing in spite of trying multiple locations, varied hours of operation and extensive advertising campaigns. However, the mobile pregnancy center was a much-loved program, particularly to this specific group of donors. We were averaging only five clients per month, many of whom did make a choice for life after seeing the ultrasound of their baby.

But after two years of operation, it became clear that the amount of money we were spending on operations and staffing of the mobile unit would be much more effectively used to expand our services by opening another center. I could not justify spending the funds in a way that did not reflect good stewardship principles. I was able show most of our donors that by opening a new center in a location close to the abortion clinic in our town, we could use those funds to see many more abortion-minded clients than we were reaching with our mobile unit.

> Some donors did not agree with the decision, but overall the result has been positive and our donor base has continued to be strong. As an added bonus to this very hard decision, we were able to find a rural area that was in need of a mobile unit and were able to gift the mobile unit to them.
>
> **—DIANE F.**

---

doing spiritual things, the mission is being accomplished. Sometimes the hardest thing for a nonprofit manager to do is to stop resourcing a nonproductive program—to "cut it down"—and redirect the resources, potentially achieving greater growth or "fruit" as a result. Without question, these are hard decisions to make and require a strong understanding of the stewardship role of management.

The parable suggests several steward leadership principles:

- Principle of growth (or return on investment): Resources exist to grow and bear fruit. If this is not occurring, resources should be redirected into other areas or applications that will produce growth.

- Principle of optimum investment: Resources sometimes take additional investment or time to produce growth, but there should be a limit to what is invested before growth must occur. Knowing that "investment limit" requires an intimate knowledge of the master's objectives, of the resources themselves and of the options available.

- Principle of risk: Sometimes investment in resources will produce growth and sometimes it will not, but loss can be mitigated through prudent risk. Failure is not necessarily a reflection on the owner or steward. It is often nothing more than a natural outcome of managing resources.

- Principle of responsibility: A steward accepts responsibility for achieving the desired results of the owner, for redirecting nonproducing resources and, if necessary, for ending nonfruitful investments.

The parable of the shrewd steward (Lk 16:1-13).

Jesus told his disciples: "There was a rich man whose manager [*oikonomon*] was accused of wasting his possessions. So he called him in and asked him,

'What is this I hear about you? Give an account of your management [*oiko-nomias*], because you cannot be manager any longer.'

"The manager said to himself, 'What shall I do now? My master is taking away my job. I'm not strong enough to dig, and I'm ashamed to beg—I know what I'll do so that, when I lose my job here, people will welcome me into their houses.'

"So he called in each one of his master's debtors. He asked the first, 'How much do you owe my master?'

"'Eight hundred gallons of olive oil,' he replied.

"The manager told him, 'Take your bill, sit down quickly, and make it four hundred.'

"Then he asked the second, 'And how much do you owe?'

"'A thousand bushels of wheat,' he replied.

"He told him, 'Take your bill and make it eight hundred.'

"The master commended the dishonest manager because he had acted shrewdly. For the people of this world are more shrewd in dealing with their own kind than are the people of the light. I tell you, use worldly wealth to gain friends for yourselves, so that when it is gone, you will be welcomed into eternal dwellings.

"Whoever can be trusted with very little can also be trusted with much, and whoever is dishonest with very little will also be dishonest with much. So if you have not been trustworthy in handling worldly wealth, who will trust you with true riches? And if you have not been trustworthy with someone else's property, who will give you property of your own?

"No servant can serve two masters. Either he will hate the one and love the other, or he will be devoted to the one and despise the other. You cannot serve both God and money." (Lk 16:1-13)

This parable is one of the most difficult parables to interpret, but it offers a rare glimpse into the scope and responsibility that might be vested in a steward by an owner. The main interpretive dilemma centers around two primary perplexities: the commendation given by the owner to his steward for acting shrewdly and Jesus' recommendation that his followers "use worldly wealth to gain friends" for themselves. Since our primary purpose is to discern a typology of the steward, we will survey the major interpretative positions of this passage only briefly while focusing more intently on what is germane to the role and responsibilities of the steward.

Jesus' parable concerns a wealthy business owner who fires his steward for wasting his assets. Knowing that a demanded accounting[12] of his stewardship is imminent, the steward quickly enacts a plan to use one last opportunity to wield his stewardly authority. He goes to each of his master's debtors and dramatically reduces their debt, thus binding his master by his actions as his legal agent while obliging to himself the future friendship and support of others. When the master learns of the steward's actions, he praises the steward for acting shrewdly (or prudently), leaving unstated the reason for this commendation. Jesus concludes his parable with a twofold application for his disciples: use worldly wealth in a similarly astute manner to further spiritual purposes, and be a trustworthy steward by managing spiritual resources in the same way one stewards earthly resources.

In what ways are the steward's actions worthy of praise by the master—and not just blatantly dishonest? Some believe the master was praising the steward's shrewdness but not his ethics. Others focus on the fact that the debts seem excessively large, either because the steward has added his own "commission" onto the debts or they have grown disproportionately because of accrued interest. Either way, the steward is restoring the debts to their previous or non-inflated values.

Once again, we observe a number of themes regarding stewardship in this parable:

- Stewards may be called to account at any time for the management of the resources under their care.

- Improper management or abuse of resources may be grounds for immediate dismissal of a steward, at times with severe consequences.

- Character qualities that are commendable in a steward are shrewdness (or prudence), trustworthiness, generosity and integrity. However, shrewdness by itself can spiral out of control and thus needs to be expressed along with other moral character traits to be appropriate.

- Trustworthiness is often tested through faithful stewardship of a small amount of resources, with greater resources as a possible reward.

- The trustworthy steward brings the same character and integrity to little or to much, to material or spiritual resources, and to personal resources or God's resources. The untrustworthy steward selectively applies character and lacks integrity. "One may think that what is 'least' does not count so that he may treat it as he pleases; but no, it is quite decisive as revealing our true character. One may think that if something very great were entrusted to him, he would be faithful; men will not agree with him, they will first want to test him out with something that is very small."[13]

- Effective stewards do not try to serve more than one master. Since the unjust steward attempts to develop multiple loyalties by endearing himself to others while still in the service of his master, Jesus pinpoints the problem by concluding, "No servant can serve two masters." These "masters" can be anything that absorbs the steward's attention or allegiance, such as alcohol, sexual indulgence, a personal business and so on.

The parable of the talents (Mt 25:14-30).

"Again, it [the kingdom] will be like a man going on a journey, who called his servants and entrusted his property to them. To one he gave five talents of money, to another two talents, and to another one talent, each according to his ability. Then he went on his journey. The man who had received the five talents went at once and put his money to work and gained five more. So also, the one with the two talents gained two more. But the man who had received the one talent went off, dug a hole in the ground and hid his master's money.

"After a long time the master of those servants returned and settled accounts with them. The man who had received the five talents brought the other five. 'Master,' he said, 'you entrusted me with five talents. See, I have gained five more.'

"His master replied, 'Well done, good and faithful servant! You have been faithful with a few things; I will put you in charge of many things. Come and share your master's happiness!'

"The man with the two talents also came. 'Master,' he said, 'you entrusted me with two talents; see, I have gained two more.'

"His master replied, 'Well done, good and faithful servant! You have been faithful with a few things; I will put you in charge of many things. Come and share your master's happiness!'

"Then the man who had received the one talent came. 'Master,' he said, 'I knew that you are a hard man, harvesting where you have not sown and gathering where you have not scattered seed. So I was afraid and went out and hid your talent in the ground. See, here is what belongs to you.'

"His master replied, 'You wicked, lazy servant! So you knew that I harvest where I have not sown and gather where I have not scattered seed? Well then, you should have put my money on deposit with the bankers, so that when I returned I would have received it back with interest.

"'Take the talent from him and give it to the one who has the ten talents. For everyone who has will be given more, and he will have an abundance. Whoever does not have, even what he has will be taken from him. And throw that worthless servant outside, into the darkness, where there will be weeping and gnashing of teeth.'" (Mt 25:14-30)

This parable—and its parallel in Luke 19:11-27—is one of the richest sources of information about the steward in the biblical record. The three individuals in this story are called *doulous* (slaves), and not the more specific *oikonomous* (stewards). However, although the specific term for steward is not employed, the master treats the servants with such clear stewardship roles that they can be considered stewards or stewards in training. Since the master assigns three different servants to manage sums of money to manage in his absence, it's possible he has not yet identified the steward of the estate and is testing potential candidates.

The wealthy master wants to see his finances invested in his absence. He thus entrusts large sums of money to the servants, giving each a different amount in accordance with his abilities. The intended purpose of the trust is for the servants to "put the money to work" while the master is gone and produce financial gain through trading or business (Mt 25:16; Lk 19:13, 15).

Upon returning "after a long time," the master asks for the expected accounting from each steward. The first two proudly display double the amount they were originally given, earning praise for being good and faithful. Their reward for a successful outcome is additional responsibility and a share in the master's happiness. The third steward, though, has taken his talent and buried it. He excuses his behavior out of fear based on his perception—whether right or wrong the parable does not tell us—of his master's harsh and unethical character. In reply, the master points out the true character of the steward, calling him wicked and lazy, and turns the tables on the steward by accusing him of not acting in accord with his perception of the master's character. If he thought the master was harsh, he should have acted accordingly and at least invested the money with a safe banker for a minimal return of interest. This lazy steward's punishment is total loss of his resources, possibly through dismissal or demotion.

It is informative to note that in Matthew 25, each servant is given different amounts of money but two produce the same one hundred percent profit margin. In the parallel Luke 19 account, each steward is given the same amount but they produce different profit margins. Jesus may have told the same story twice but with different emphases. The story as told in Matthew stresses different starting abilities resulting in different levels of stewardship responsibility, while the Luke parallel stresses different outcomes, resulting in different future advancements. Both emphases are important aspects of stewardship.

Three separate Greek words used in these passages reveal different aspects of the master's goals for the stewards' work: (1) *ergazomai*, "to work, trade," is used in Matthew 25:16, (2) *pragmateuomai*, "to conduct or be engaged in a business," is used in Luke 19:13 and (3) *diapragmateuomai*, "to gain by trading, to earn," is used in Luke 19:15. All three words emphasize a common commercial focus of first-century stewards. They stress how the master wanted the stewards to make the resources grow: (1) by putting the resources "to work" (since money by itself is a non-working asset), (2) by using resources to conduct business or trade and (3) by using resources to create financial growth.

This story is very germane to modern nonprofit management. I have seen nonprofit leaders get caught in the trap of thinking their primary role was to "sustain" or "take care of" the resources of the organization when in fact the stakeholders were looking for growth, investment into new areas or greater impact.

Valuable observations about potential roles and responsibilities of the steward occur throughout this parable:

- Fulfilling the master's expectations is the primary goal of stewardship, which in many cases involves the expectation of growth or gain in assets. In this particular case, the two stewards are praised for applying themselves to growing the talents, while the specific amount they were able to gain seemed of secondary importance.

HOW AS A STEWARD LEADER I NOW THINK DIFFERENTLY ABOUT ENDOWMENTS

Endowments seem to be an essential part of many nonprofits' funding strategies these days and are considered one of the few ways a nonprofit can ensure sustainability. Endowments tend to be solicited primarily by colleges and universities (Harvard leads the pack with a whopping $32 billion endowment), although now even smaller nonprofits are trying to raise endowments to fund everything from capital improvements to program funds. If an endowment is managed carefully, it can fund specific programs and needs in perpetuity.

But are endowments good stewardship? I'm not sure. On one hand, endowments are possible because there are donors who want their donation used to produce sustainable results year after year. So an endowment can be considered the faithful management of a stakeholder's resources according to their objectives and desires. Most would agree that it is prudent to put some resources aside for "a rainy day," so what's the difference between a small savings account and a multi-billion-dollar endowment except in scope? If I were running a nonprofit that had a large endowment, I would probably enjoy the security of knowing there was a predictable source of annual funding that I didn't have to raise anew every year.

But it seems hard to reconcile endowments with certain biblical principles. The story told by Jesus about the rich man in Luke 12:13-21 warns against the false security that hoarding provides, and in 2 Corinthians 8:13-15 we are encouraged to view the "plenty" we have today as a provision from God, the owner of all resources, to provide for today's needs in others (not tomorrow's needs). When endowments become our security instead of trust in the Lord, we are reminded by birds who keep nothing in store not to lose sight of the joy of depending on God for the resources we need (Mt 6:25-34).

Endowments are a stewardship issue. As steward leaders we need to be careful not to view the resources God gives us as an entitlement that will always be there or as a crutch that can divert us from an intimate and dependent relationship with the Master.

So I'm not a fan of endowments. I can accept how Bible-believing Christians can make a biblical case for endowments. But I also know how hard it is to maintain a focus of dependence on God when lots of money is involved.

- Stewards should not view resources as static or as assets just to be maintained. Many resources are inactive and need to be wisely "put to work," invested, applied or converted to other resources for growth.[14]

- Prudent risk can be a necessary and unavoidable aspect of stewardship. It is the master's responsibility to define the level of acceptable risk, not the steward. However, risk avoidance may be necessary under certain circumstances to protect the asset as long as it is not motivated by fear or laziness.

- The manner in which a steward fulfills his or her responsibilities can be based on any number of criteria: the content of any direct instructions from the master, the steward's prior experience or skill, the confidence and expectation of the master-owner in the steward's ability to perform, or the steward's knowledge and understanding of the master's character, expectations and goals.

- Stewards and masters should experience a reciprocal relationship that involves—at least to some degree—mutual awareness, understanding of one another, mutual reward and mutual participation in the fruits of growth.

- The master has the right to judge performance based on a steward's potential to perform. The master is interested in what could have been done given proper instruction and assessment of the skills of the steward.

- Stewards are singularly accountable to the master-owner. Each steward's work is judged on its own merit and results.

- A steward focuses primarily on his responsibilities while the master focuses on his rights—not vice versa. Randy Alcorn summarizes this significant distinction between the master and steward: "As stewards our rights are limited by our lack of ownership. Instead, we manage assets for the owner's benefit, and we carry no sense of entitlement to the assets we manage. It's our job to find out what the owner wants done with his assets, then carry out his will. If we focus on the master's rights, we will fulfill our responsibilities. But the moment we begin to focus on what we think we deserve, on what we think our master or others owe us, we lose perspective. The quality of our service deteriorates rapidly."[15]

- Stewards are often entrusted with wider service and greater responsibility as they demonstrate faithfulness and success in accomplishing the goals of the master.

Major stewardship themes in the parables. Let's review several of the repeated themes in the parables of Jesus that are most germane to the steward.

Character matters. The moral character of the steward is often highlighted in the historical sources, but none more so than in the parabolic teachings of Jesus. Character plays a pivotal role in virtually every stewardship parable told by Jesus. The essential character traits necessary for successful stewardship are repeatedly illustrated: faithfulness, wisdom, responsibility, integrity and trustworthiness. As if to emphasize the point, Jesus paints contrasting pictures of stewards whose behavior hinge on differences in moral character in several of the parables (Lk 12:42-48; 16:10-12; Mt 25:14-30). Although other writers may talk about character, Jesus clearly makes it one of the central determinants of good behavior through his teachings concerning the link between inner character and outward behavior: "The things that come out of the mouth come from the heart, and these make a man unclean" (Mt 15:18), and "The good man brings good things out of the good stored up in him, and the evil man brings evil things out of the evil stored up in him" (Mt 12:35).

Stewards must give an account for their stewardship. To have resources placed in one's trust implies that there will be an accounting of that trust at some point in time. As we have seen in many of the parables on stewardship, even in the first century there was an established process for accountability

HOW I LEARNED TO PAY MORE ATTENTION TO CHARACTER THAN COMPETENCE

For about ten years in the eighties and early nineties, my wife Laurie and I worked in church planting and leadership development in Portugal. For the last six of those years I led an old, traditional church and helped it reinvent itself into a more dynamic, outward-reaching congregation. Laurie and I worked hard and put in long hours, but we also relaxed and enjoyed the ebb and flow of Portugal's "café culture." God did some remarkable things in the church, in its city and in the outlying small towns where we also formed deep, lifelong friendships.

Our time with that church came to an end because I was asked by my organization to come back to the home office and take on a new leadership role. After much agonizing, talking with mentors and prayer, we decided it was God's next step for us. We and our friends shed tears as we tore ourselves away. As befits the Portuguese way of doing things, a solemn goodbye dinner was organized.

During the dinner person after person got up and reflected on our time among them and what God had done in our midst. What they talked about and what they did not mention struck us profoundly and has marked us to this day.

No one mentioned the sermons, the radio programs on the local station, the training institute for church leaders, the preaching points, the Bible studies, the reorganization of the kids' ministry, the outreach events in the town square, the—well, you get the picture. No one mentioned the activities and tasks into which we had all poured so much time and effort.

What they did talk about was watching Laurie and me—how we treated each other and how we parented our three kids. Church members talked about how we related to them and their friends and neighbors. They told stories about how we handled ourselves during turbulent times as we changed the church culture and old mindsets. In short, they talked about who we were and our character. That was their focus during that solemn goodbye dinner, when time was short and words were carefully chosen.

Their perspective hit us hard. All those activities we worked so hard at were important and God used them. But our character—simply who we were and how that revealed itself—was much more important and was the medium through which God had done his deepest work.

—BRUCE S.

by the steward to the master. Such accounting generally involved a review of the state of the resources, an inspection of the records of receipts and payments of money and materials, and records of total crop or production yield. This accounting process was relatively simple and existed primarily to keep accurate records of production and expose any losses due to theft or negligence (modern approaches to accounting that calculated profit and loss did not exist in antiquity).

The concept of the steward was instrumental in the development of the principles and practices of today's financial accounting and corporate accountability. Even though this accountability took a simple form in the first century, it was central to the relationship between steward and master and only increased in its sophistication through the centuries. The earliest records of stewards address two fundamental questions of accountability: To whom is the steward accountable, and for what is the steward accountable? The essential nature of accountability hasn't changed over the centuries. These two questions still guide corporate and nonprofit accountability today. The answer to the first question has always been the same: stewards are accountable to the owner of the resources (whether explicit or implicit). However, the answer to the second question has changed over the centuries: the extent and scope of what stewards are accountable for has changed as greater accountability has been required.

Stewardship involves relationship. Stewardship in its base form implies responsibility, trusteeship and accountability. A steward can fulfill his or her responsibilities with only a cognitive knowledge of the master's intentions and desires. But the concept of stewardship as it is developed in the New Testament goes far beyond this base expectation to include the idea of intimacy and even relationship with the master (Mt 25:21; Eph 1:17; 4:13; Col 1:9). Biblical stewardship involves relationship on several different levels. Scott Rodin calls the biblical steward "a wholly relational term" that is developed in the Bible on four relational levels:

- The steward and the owner: The biblical steward does not just know about the owner—he must also know the owner's character, wishes and desires.

- The steward and the recipients: The biblical steward invests the resources of the owner in the lives of those to whom the owner is inclined and thus exercises care for both the resources and those who will benefit from the resources (see Lk 12:42-43).

- The steward and self: Rodin's understanding of the steward's relationship with himself is supported by the parabolic stories that reveal the extent to which the steward is free to supply his own needs from the master's resources: "There is a relationship between the steward and the steward's own needs. That is, while the resources are not owned by the steward, the steward is expected to live from the resources and in that way be a steward to himself or herself. There is a self-stewardship implied in the term."[16]

- The steward and the resources themselves: Rather than give in to the temptation to exploit or waste resources, the biblical steward refuses to act as owner himself and exercises the same caretaking, investing and application exhibited by the owner of the resources (see Gen 1:28-30; 2:15).[17]

A common goal of stewardship is to grow resources. The ultimate goal of stewardship is determined by the owner of the resources. Some owners may want their steward to sustain their resources, keeping them intact, healthy and functioning (as in the case of livestock). However, in a number of the parables we see owners looking for growth in their resources through fruit-bearing, capital growth (business) or multiplication (agriculture). The parable of the talents illustrates this principle three ways: (1) through the detailed instructions given by the master to the stewards—the three verbal instructions, (2) in the praise given to the two stewards who grew the money entrusted to them and (3) in the condemnation of the third steward who didn't even grow his money through interest.

Growth in the resources can take on many forms depending on the nature of the resource. If the resource is people, growth can be measured in efficiency, effectiveness, skill development, commitment and longevity. If the resource is troubled teens (as in a nonprofit organization), growth can be measured in changed lives or social impact. If the resource is raw materials, growth comes from greater efficiency of production or higher value in the finished product.

People who manage resources in the corporate world seem to naturally understand this objective of stewardship. They know that growth in revenue, profit, efficiency and/or equity is key to meeting the objectives of owners or stockholders. I've observed that nonprofit executives have more trouble with this concept. Their aversion to growth may come from a variety of sources: self-protection, the fear of risk, a misguided notion that "not-for-profit" means no growth or profit, or the challenges of measuring missional impact. Nonprofit organizational leaders should heed the encouragement of stakeholders if they make it obvious that they want to see their donor dollars produce increased impact, self-generating capital, value-added services or social capital.

Faithful stewards advance. Another theme common to many of Jesus' parables of stewardship is the promise of advancement for the faithful steward (Lk 12:42-48; 16:10-12; Mt 25:14-30). Faithful stewardship of a small resource is often rewarded with greater responsibility, and trustworthy stewardship of material resources can result in the stewardship of immaterial or spiritual resources (Lk 16:11). Although the parables of Jesus do not directly highlight differences in the stewardship of material resources compared with the stewardship of human resources, Jesus' lack of differentiation seems to imply that the same principles of good stewardship and advancement apply to both. For Jesus, faithfulness and advancement are important aspects of the steward's hope and progress.

HOW I INSTILLED THE VALUE OF GROWTH AS GOOD STEWARDSHIP

NavPress Publishing was one of the nonprofit organizations I was blessed to be able to lead for more than a decade. It was a missional publishing house staffed with people who worked there because they believed in the power of words to transform people's lives. Mission was always more important than money, but I knew that if there was no money, there would be no mission.

The businessman in me wanted to see NavPress grow in revenue so we could do more publishing and be more stable. But I quickly learned that the NavPress staff were not motivated by the idea of year-over-year revenue growth. They didn't even get very excited about growth in the number of books we published. What did excite them was stories of lives that were changed through our books.

As a former electrical engineer, I was comfortable with numbers. But growth in things one could easily count (such as money, books and sales) caused most people to glaze over. So I took a personal retreat for the express purpose of trying to hear from God what his vision was for NavPress that would excite and motivate others. I felt that it needed to be a vision of growth, but growth in what way?

What I heard that weekend was that God had given us a unique stewardship through the resources of books and magazines to change people's lives to become more like Christ. Our stewardship was in the organic, spiritual growth of people who were reached with the message of salvation, discipled in the Word and equipped to serve a needy world.

But how could we measure growth in people's lives like we measured money or books produced? Not as easily, but even spiritual growth can be measured to some degree. The apostle Paul could tell the difference between spiritual babes and mature believers (Heb 5:11-14). So we set about trying to assess the spiritual impact of the books we produced through various means. We asked the authors to clarify the type of spiritual growth they intended through their writing. We collected readers' stories, counted the number of readers who came back for more resources, measured "pass-along" readership and developed other indicators of spiritual growth. No longer were we happy to just "publish books." We wanted to change the world.

THE STEWARD IN THE EPISTLES

In the Old Testament we find a primarily non-theological use of the term *oikonomos* as the chief servant of a household or a governmental officer. Foundational truths—such as the image of God in man and God's ownership of all creation—form a basis for understanding stewardship, but the theological implications are not fully developed until the New Testament. The parabolic teachings of Jesus emphasize the character qualities of the steward and correlate faithfulness in the material world with increased responsibilities in the spiritual or future world.

However, not until the writings of the apostle Paul and the other apostles in the Epistles is there full development of the theological and metaphorical meaning of the work of the steward as stewardship (*oikonomia*). Since the focus of our study is the person and role of the biblical steward and not the theology of stewardship, we will primarily study how the Pauline Epistles elaborate on the person of the steward. Two major themes emerge from Paul's letters: the vast spheres of stewardship and the centrality of the serving steward.

The spheres of stewardship. A steward can be given management responsibility of almost any resource owned by another person. Christian writings of the last century have focused on the stewardship of "time, talents and treasures," but many more spheres are illustrated in the Bible, especially in Paul's letters. The following list summarizes the breadth of Paul's understanding of stewardship:

- stewardship of time
- stewardship of abilities (talents)

- stewardship of money

- stewardship of community

- stewardship of natural resources (creation)

- stewardship of power or dominion

- stewardship of material resources (possessions)

- stewardship of spiritual realities (the gospel)

- stewardship of spiritual gifts

- stewardship of grace

- stewardship of relationships

- stewardship of the poor and disenfranchised

- stewardship of self (mind, will, emotions)

- stewardship of our bodies

- stewardship of God's image (*imago Dei*)

- the serving steward

Even though the core identity of the biblical steward was that of a slave or servant, most biblical expositors overlook this foundational identity or give it only cursory affirmation. Jesus affirms it: "I am among you as one who serves" (Lk 22:27). Paul equally acknowledges that his stewardship comes in the form of service: "Men ought to regard us as servants of Christ and those entrusted with [stewards of] the secret things of God" (1 Cor 4:1). Scott Rodin reminds us that the work of a steward is the work of a servant: "We are stewards here only as we participate in Christ in his work as the faithful servant of God. This participation is the work of the steward."[18] It is important to point out that the reverse of this statement is not necessarily true ("the work of a servant is the work of a steward"). Said differently, all stewards are servants but not all servants are stewards. Even though Peter Block wrote a nonreligious business book on stewardship, he affirms this biblical premise when he relates how service is central to stewardship:

> To hold something of value in trust calls for placing service ahead of control,
> to no longer expect leaders to be in charge and out in front. There is pride in

leadership, it evokes images of direction. There is humility in stewardship, it evokes images of service. Service is central to the idea of stewardship.[19]

In this chapter we developed from the biblical record an exegetical and historical study of the steward and stewardship. We focused on the characteristics of the steward in the Old Testament era, the parables of Jesus and the Pauline Epistles in the New Testament. Our main purpose has been to articulate a typology of the characteristics and responsibilities of the biblical steward. We analyzed the Hebrew and Greek words used in the Bible to describe the steward and stewardship, exegeted the primary Old Testament and New Testament passages that illustrate the steward in ancient Semitic and Christian life, and have drawn general conclusions from the biblical observations.

We now turn our attention to pulling all of what we have learned concerning the historical steward into a contemporary description and model of the steward leader.

SECTION TWO

The STEWARD LEADERSHIP MODEL

We are now ready to look at what steward leadership means for those who lead organizations. Steward leadership is distinct from other leadership models in that it has unique purposes, it presupposes that non-ownership of resources affects how one leads, it is based on the identity of the leader as a steward and a servant, and it clarifies the impact of the relationship between the owner of the resources and the steward leader. To help unpack how steward leadership is distinct from other leadership models, we will compare it to its closest "cousin," the servant leadership model. Finally, we will see how steward leadership matures over time through four distinct stages.

4

The Steward Leadership Model

Mark was in an executive leadership role in a Christian publishing association for the very first time. He had held senior leadership positions in other organizations, but somehow this new role seemed different to him. Maybe it was because the buck stopped with him this time, or because this organization was an association of Christian publishing companies.

Whatever the reason, Mark felt an automatic and compelling responsibility to the publishers who were members of his organization and for whom his organization existed. His predecessor had sometimes run the organization like he knew better than the members what they needed. But Mark emphasized to the staff a core message from day one: "We need to remember that we are here because of our members. Our purpose is to find out what they need and try to accomplish it for them in the most cost-effective manner."

Time was carved out in each staff member's schedule to spend time talking with the members, and Mark devoted an inordinate amount of time traveling between publishing houses and listening to the concerns of the publishers. He had never read a book on steward leadership, but instinctively he knew he was accountable to his members and was managing financial resources given to the organization to accomplish their goals. He was a steward at heart.

Stewards played significant roles in history, economics, religion and commerce for millennia, and they are still all around us today. They may not necessarily present themselves as such. As we noted earlier, a steward is anyone who manages property and resources belonging to another in order to achieve the owner's objectives. With this understanding of the role, we can find stewards in almost every sector of life:

- people who manage companies on behalf of their owners
- people who manage publicly traded companies
- politicians and civil servants
- people who serve the country in the military
- parents, foster parents and legal guardians
- financial and legal trustees
- educators
- people of faith who believe they are stewards of God's resources
- people who work in nonprofit organizations

If stewards are all around us, and if each of us serves a steward at one time or another in life (if not every day), how would our leadership change if we formulated our role around that of the steward? In chapter one I argued that most current leadership models are insufficient to address all of the challenges faced by those who lead nonprofit organizations. The same can be said for leaders of any other type of organization—from a business to the military—if those leaders see themselves as stewards.

I propose, then, this general definition of organizational steward leadership: *Steward leadership is the efficient management and growth of organizational resources, through leadership of staff and activities as a non-owning steward-servant, in order to achieve the mission according to the objectives of the owners.* This definition of steward leadership emphasizes five important concepts: (1) the two main purposes of stewarding resources are efficiency and growth, (2) the individual is both managing (resources) and leading/influencing (people), (3) the leader does not own the resources under management, (4) the identity of the leader is that of a steward and a servant, and (5) achieving the objectives of the owners is the ultimate goal. When applied to specific spheres of steward leadership, the definition can be modified accordingly:

- For faith-based organizations, substitute "God and the stakeholders" for "the owners."
- For leaders of publicly traded companies, substitute "stockholders" for "owners."

- For politicians, substitute "public resources and services" for "organizational resources" and "constituents" for "owners."

- For military leaders, substitute "defense resources" for "organizational resources" and "citizens" for "owners."

- For nonprofit organizational leaders, substitute "stakeholders" for "owners."

With this definition in hand, we can now unpack the core foundations on which steward leadership exists, the distinctive characteristics of the steward leader and the range of resources a steward leader might oversee. We'll start with a brief history of steward leadership, addressing where the leadership model comes from and its contributors.

A SHORT HISTORY OF THE STEWARD LEADERSHIP MODEL

Our history of steward leadership begins with those who wrote about stewardship and leadership in general without calling it an extant model. Andrew Coleman, Larry Spears and Lewis Solomon all have referred to stewardship as one of many attributes or values of a leader. Other well-known writers have referred to the leader as steward but have scarcely developed the concept. In *Leadership Is an Art*, Max De Pree is one of the earliest contemporary writers to address the idea: "The art of leadership requires us to think about the leader-as-steward in terms of relationships: of assets and legacy, of momentum and effectiveness, of civility and values."[1] However, because of his respect for Robert Greenleaf (the "father" of servant leadership), when De Pree speaks of stewardship, he generally means servanthood and does not develop the concept with any detail. Peter Senge also speaks briefly of the leader as steward, but his development of the model extends only to a leader's sense of purpose and destiny and becoming "a steward of the vision."[2]

The history of those who directly propose or elaborate a model of steward leadership is a short history, starting only in 1989. Robert Clinton, a professor of leadership at Fuller Theological Seminary, appears to be the first to briefly articulate the stewardship model as one of four main leadership models in the Bible (alongside the harvest model, shepherd model and servant model). Clinton considers the stewardship model (or the accountability model, as he alternately calls it) "the most foundational of all four models" in that it applies to all leaders regardless of gifting. "The stewardship model is a philosophical model which is founded on the central thrust of several accountability passages [in the Bible], that is, that a leader must give an account of his/her ministry to God."[3] Clinton defines eight basic values that support the steward leadership model as it is applied to Christian leaders:

- Ministry challenges, tasks and assignments ultimately come from God.

- God holds a leader accountable for leadership influence and for growth and conduct of followers.

- There will be an ultimate accounting of a leader to God for one's performance in leadership.

- Leaders will receive rewards for faithfulness to their ministry in terms of abilities, skills, gifts and opportunities.

- Leaders are expected to build on abilities, skills and gifts so as to maximize potential.

- Leaders will be uniquely gifted (both as to gifts and the degree to which the gift can be used effectively).

- Leaders will receive rewards for their productivity as they zealously use their abilities, skills, gifts and opportunities for God.

- Leaders must hold to higher standards than followers due to the "above reproach" and "modeling" impact.[4]

In a paper presented at the International Faith and Learning Seminar in Australia in 1993, David Birkenstock briefly explains the unique qualities of "Christian leadership." He initially identifies the servant leadership model as the "most distinctive contribution from Christian literature," but because of negative connotations associated with servant leadership, he commends the term *steward* as "a biblical term that would more clearly identify the Christian leader without the negative connotations of servant.... The concept of steward leadership more closely suits the idea of Christian leadership. It incorporates the idea of servanthood and more fully recognizes the role of manager and of being fully accountable, responsible and reliable."[5] Unfortunately, Birkenstock does not develop the concept of the steward leader any further.

Peter Block applies stewardship to corporate leadership next in his seminal 1993 book *Stewardship: Choosing Service over Self-Interest*. In this mostly theoretical book, Block views stewardship as a more effective concept for what is normally understood as leadership. To Block, stewardship equals empowerment, giving employees at all levels choice over how to serve customers by leading with an attitude of service rather than control (in other words, by redistributing power, purpose and wealth). A weakness in Block's definition of stewardship is that it is so strongly biased toward servanthood and the redistribution of power that the leader retains very little legitimate power or authority in the end—just service to those with redistributed power:

> Stewardship is defined in this book as the choice to preside over the orderly distribution of power. This means giving people at the bottom and the boundaries of the organization choice over how to serve a customer, a citizen, a community. It is the willingness to be accountable for the well-being of the larger organization by operating in service, rather than in control, of those around us. Stated simply, it is accountability without control or compliance.[6]

He also takes generic leadership to task by polarizing it and stewardship against one another:

> The alternative to leadership is stewardship. Not a perfect concept, but an entryway into exploring what fundamental, sustainable change in our organizations would look like. Stewardship asks us to be deeply accountable for the outcomes of an institution, without acting to define purpose for others, control others, or take care of others. Stewardship can be most simply defined as giving order to the dispersion of power. It requires us to systematically move choice and resources closer and closer to the bottom and edges of the organization. Leadership, in contrast, gives order to the centralization of power. It keeps choices and resources at the center and places power at the boundaries as an exception to be earned.[7]

Block develops his unique approach to the leader as steward by elaborating on four contrasting pairs of skills. His first contrast has already been stated, namely, choosing stewardship over leadership. Block faults leadership, as he sees it most often expressed, as the ineffective localization of power, purpose and privilege in the leader. Second, Block recommends choosing partnership (or the distribution of power and ownership) over patriarchy. However, classical approaches to stewardship involve the recognition that ownership resides completely outside of all managers and employees and is not merely spread around. His third and least-developed contrast involves choosing empowerment over dependency. Empowerment involves trusting people to know best what needs to be done for the customer, giving them responsibility and the power to define purpose for themselves. Block wraps up all of his contrasts by recommending service over self-interest. The rest of his book examines what these service-based governance strategies look like in management practices and structures, staff functions, financial practices, compensation and performance evaluation.

Block's contribution to an understanding of the steward leader is fresh and unique in corporate literature. His emphasis on service, empowerment and accountability resides at the heart of classical stewardship. His understanding of the permeating nature of true stewardship and its effect on management practices, staff functions and human resources demonstrates the breadth with which he sees stewardship impacting an organization. However, his narrow definitions of leadership and power bias his understanding of the role of the steward as leader and set him up for an either/or view of corporate governance instead of both/and.

In 1996 Richard Higginson wrote about transforming leadership as the practical outworking of Christian discipleship, and in the process identified three biblical images of a leader: servant, shepherd and steward. He then relates all three to management and leadership. Speaking briefly about the image of the steward, Higginson says, "It may well be that this is therefore an image more for managers than leaders! Yet as soon as one says that, one must qualify it, because the essence of stewardship is accountability: being accountable to one's master for the management of resources. Leaders too are accountable, though exactly who they answer to varies widely."[8] Like other early writers who refer to the steward leader, Higginson doesn't develop the model further.

In Richard Daft's 1999 textbook on leadership models there is a rare but brief reference to the role of steward leadership under the heading of moral leadership. According to Daft, the growth in acceptance of moral leadership "encourages change toward developing followers into leaders, thereby developing their potential rather than using leadership position to control or limit followers."[9] Stewardship results from the pivotal shift in leadership thinking from authoritarianism to service. Unfortunately, Daft largely follows the lead of Block in his brief reference to this leadership model.

HOW I FIRST LEARNED WHAT IT MEANT TO LEAD LIKE A STEWARD

As a lifetime educator and devoted follower of Jesus Christ, I have served my entire career in various K-12 school, church, university and nonprofit organizational roles ranging from teacher, superintendent, elder and vice president to president and board member. My desire has always been to lead like Jesus Christ led because I believe he is the best teacher and leader the world has ever known! I was familiar with Robert Greenleaf's work on servant leadership, and his theoretical basis along with my understanding of Scripture provided the foundation for my understanding of biblical leadership—that is until one summer in 2006 when I was asked to teach a course on stewardship to doctoral students at a major Christian university.

To prepare for this course, I chose as textbooks *Stewardship: Choosing Service over Self-Interest* by Block (1993) and *Nonprofit Stewardship* by Brinckerhoff (2004). I then set out to discover what the Bible taught about steward leadership. I studied the parable of the talents and the story of Joseph, and I was particularly impacted by Scriptures such as 1 Chronicles 29:10-13 and Psalm 24:1. Later, I read Kent Wilson's dissertation and came across the concept that in the Bible "all stewards are servants, but not all servants are stewards." It dawned on me that the difference was in the attitude of the heart!

At that moment I decided to live my life as a faithful steward committed to fulfilling the purposes of my Master for all he has entrusted into my care. A few years later I substituted Scott Rodin's book *The Steward Leader* (2010) for the Block text, and today I teach steward leadership as the foundational biblical construct of leadership for all of the leadership classes I teach in my current role as a university professor.

—**BRIAN S.**

Peter Brinckerhoff in 2004 introduces the first full-length analysis of stewardship in nonprofit organizations. He begins with an explanation of the steward that is the closest to the definition of the classic steward of any research source we have reviewed so far:

> The stewardship philosophy of leadership . . . reminds us that the not-for-profit sector organizations actually belong to the communities they serve, and leaders have temporary stewardship over their assets. The key concept here is this: as a steward, your job is to manage your not-for-profit with the same care, the same attention to detail, the same level of responsibility that you would give to someone else's property—because that's the reality. "Your" not-for-profit is not, in actuality, yours; it really belongs to the community and you are but the temporary steward of its resources. While many of us take justifiable pride in "our" organization, "our" staff, "our" board, and of course "our" mission, in far too many cases "our" becomes "my" in more ways than just as a descriptor, and soon the organization loses its mission-first focus.[10]

Given such a solid beginning, Brinckerhoff loses his edge quickly and reverts to general business advice, which dominates the rest of the book. The author has moments of insight when he speaks of board members and funders as stewards, but for all other nonprofit staff roles, his understanding of stewardship comes across as generic. For example, when defining the unique role supervisors play as stewards, he says, "As stewards, supervisors understand that management is, at its core, a support function, not one of command."[11] When defining the eight "unique" qualities of the nonprofit steward leader, he lists qualities that are found on most lists of leadership traits: balance, humility, accountability, integrity, the ability to motivate, a thirst for innovation, communication skills and a quest for lifelong learning.[12]

Still, Brinckerhoff's book does significantly contribute to the study of steward leadership. His practical approach to how stewards make decisions results in a useful decision-making tool. In that tool he combines missional accountability with concern for stakeholders and appropriately engages risk in the process. Brinckerhoff also provides a unique organizational stewardship assessment tool that rates a nonprofit organization along nine characteristics.

Finally, in the latest and most detailed treatment of the steward leader, Scott Rodin in 2010 acknowledges that his Christian approach is not a "how" book on leadership, but a "who" book on the personal transformation of godly stewards who are also called to be a leaders: "We are first called to be godly stewards and then to be leaders. Commitment to our call as stewards guides us as steward leaders. But we are stewards first. It is as stewards who undergo the daily transformation of the Holy Spirit that we are sometimes called to lead."[13] According to Rodin, this process of personal transformation rests on three foundations: (1) the purpose of our existence rooted in the image of God that we bear, (2) the radical freedom the steward experiences to work in joyful, responsive obedience, and (3) the distinctiveness of the steward leader model that is based on inward-outward transformation and an emphasis on being over doing.

Rodin spends the bulk of his book evaluating the transformation process that every steward leader must go through. This process occurs simultaneously at four levels of relationship: the steward's relationship with God, with self, with others and with God's creation. Each relational transformation takes the steward on a journey—or trajectory, as Rodin calls it—that impacts the people the steward serves and the organization the steward leads. The author defines eight specific impacts that come from the transformation process:

- Steward leaders are united with the people they serve.
- Steward leaders cultivate culture.
- Steward leaders develop whole people.
- Steward leaders harness the power of people.
- Steward leaders build and value community as its own end.
- Steward leaders are caretakers of their communities.
- Steward leaders marshal resources effectively.
- Steward leaders create organizational consistency and witness.

Throughout Rodin contrasts the behavior and effectiveness of the steward leader with what he calls the owner-leader who is focused on control (rather than freedom), doing (rather than being) and leading (rather than obeying). He includes a unique section that compares the steward leader approach to other approaches to leadership such as transformational leadership, leadership and the new science, and servant leadership.

Rodin's work is the most foundational and applicable of those we have examined to the current understanding of the steward leader. He provides theological and philosophical underpinnings for understanding the steward leader's identity and internal transformational process. His emphasis on the steward's engagement with the four relational levels is original and crucial to developing a holistic model of steward leadership. Although Rodin eschews discussing leadership traits or characteristics (due to his selective focus on the process of steward transformation), his work is not antithetical to steward leadership because of the theological and basal purpose of his work.

This concludes our review of sources currently available on steward leadership. The field is sparse at best, but some foundational books have opened the way for a more situated and consistent development of stewardship as a model for leadership. On the positive side, current research on steward leadership does stress the following distinct contributions to existing leadership theory:

- There is a breadth of resources that one stewards (money, gifts, people, mission and so on).

- The steward leader has a unique service mindset toward both the owner of the resources and toward his or her followers.

- Steward leaders hold themselves accountable to owners, stakeholders and the community for how they manage the resources entrusted to them.

- Steward leadership can be seen as a form of moral leadership.

- The identity and transformation of the steward are important preconditions to leadership.

However, because research on steward leadership is still in its infancy, significant deficiencies and gaps in knowledge still exist in the current sources:

- There is a general lack of agreement on a definition of steward leadership.

- There is a general failure to recognize the importance of the relationship between the steward leader and the owner of the resources (for example, God, the community, stakeholders) as a critical determinant of the steward's priorities and accountability.

- Confusion exists among some between the servant leader and steward leader models.

- Stewardship is sometimes associated primarily with service and empowerment of others.

- Confusion exists among some who associate stewardship with management but not leadership.

- There is failure to recognize the importance of stewardship as an identity and not just a role.

- Descriptions of steward leader characteristics are limited.

- There has been little development to date of the principles and practices of leading as a steward.

THE FOUNDATIONAL LENSES OF STEWARD LEADERSHIP

The proposition of this book is that steward leadership is different from any other model of leadership and is not merely a restating of some models (such as servant leadership) or a subset of others (such as transformational leadership). In order to establish this proposition, we will start by defining the most elemental aspects of the steward leadership model. Like an optical lens that focuses attention on a specific subject, steward leadership focuses leadership through three fundamental lenses: the lens of ownership, the lens of motivation and the lens of accountability. Each lens creates its own understanding of how leadership is exercised and applied.

The lens of ownership. The lens of ownership focuses the steward leader's perspective on the rights and purposes of the owner of the resources. If there is a legal owner of resources, then he or she has full right and privilege to manage and use the resources to accomplish whatever he or she desires within the constraints of law and morality. If the owner of the resources is a different person from the one to whom the resources have been entrusted, the latter person is an agent or a steward of the owner. If an organizational leader is viewed as an agent, then agency theory assumes he or she is motivated by self-interested opportunism and strong governance structures and incentives need to be imposed by the owner to safeguard his or her rights. No special relationship or understanding is needed between owner and agent because structure and contract are imposed to ensure proper behavior. But if the organizational leader is viewed as a steward, then stewardship

HOW I NAVIGATE MY ACCOUNTABILITY TO GOD AND TO HUMAN STAKEHOLDERS

God is the ultimate owner of our mission. As the founder and leader of a nonprofit, I along with our stakeholders have tried to hear him as we have articulated that mission.

In my experience, it's often easier to articulate the mission than to know how to accomplish it. Our multiple stakeholders bring a wide range of experiences and relationships with the organization and one another. Large geographic distances separate us. Discerning how best to confidently fulfill the mission with these competing human voices makes a complex task even more challenging. Especially in our early years, I heard some stakeholders calling us to think bigger or to be more aggressive while others advised a less aggressive approach. I found it taxing to discern where God our owner would have us move. As the steward point leader, I experienced personal anxiety over the wisest way to move forward.

One of the most memorable examples occurred in 2007, our third year of ministry, a year of much confidence on our part and a year before the recession of 2008. I was assertively asking our stakeholders for input, seeking to understand how best to expand our reach. Stakeholders who were not using our materials offered few ideas, nor held strong opinions. But stakeholders who also used our products suggested we focus on providing our customers tools to help them recruit others to participate and grow spiritually. So we decided to develop and print posters, postcards and two-minute promotional videos around three of our products to follow through on their suggestion.

We put a lot of energy and funds into developing, producing and manufacturing large quantities of these promotional pieces. Yet we found little interest in using these attractive pieces. I am still not sure why. It could have been shifting moods with the shifting economy. Perhaps we did not promote our promotional materials well. Now seven years later, most of these posters, postcards and DVDs have gone into the trash with a few saved to remind us of this costly lesson.

That experience taught me several lessons that guide my accountability to both God and to human stakeholders:

- God is definitely the owner and stakeholders are implicit owners.
- While I as the point leader and the stakeholders are in a sense co-stewards, I am ultimately responsible for decisions and actions in the best interests of the owner and cannot hide behind the passion of the stakeholders.
- It is important for me as the point leader to be patient. With stakeholders, who may have only an acquaintance with one another and limited experiences and relationships with the organization, discerning direction can be complicated.
- I owe it to God, the master owner, to be prudent with vision, time, focus, personnel and capital resources.
- It is prudent to first test any direction or project on a small scale, with low risk, and expand only after it has met or surpassed expectations.
- When a stakeholder is passionate about a direction, idea or action step, we need to first experiment by spending limited energy and resources and then carefully measuring the risk. If the results are at or beyond expectations, then we expand.

—MIKE J.

theory assumes that managers have an intrinsic desire to maximize organizational performance because of a sense of duty, altruism or identification with the owners, the organization and the mission. In stewardship theory, a relationship of identification and understanding is assumed between the owner and the steward. Later in this chapter we will compare agency and stewardship theory in more detail.

One of the greatest challenges we experience as steward leaders of nonprofit organizations is trying to understand who the implicit owner or owners are and their rights and goals for the organization. Many of the nonprofit directors I have interviewed over the years found it challenging to correctly identify "ownership" in their organizations. For the most part, no one needs to tell us that we don't own the nonprofit resources we manage. We instinctively know that someone else or some other group has the right of ownership. But identifying who they are is a challenge for many.

As a Christian, I believe that God owns everything. I have tried to lead and steward nonprofit organizations being cognizant of his ownership and rights. Like many of the Christian nonprofit organizational leaders I interviewed, I was motivated by obedience to God's will and his inevitable "Well done, good and faithful servant." Scott Rodin calls this dependent humility: "The sole responsibility of the steward leader is joyous, responsive obedience."[14] But I also believe the nonprofit organization has human "implicit owners" defined as stakeholders. God owns everything that I see and have, but in the nonprofit world human "owners" also exist that have an implicit claim on the organization. God has seen fit to speak to us through the Bible and other human beings. The challenge has always been to identify which human stakeholders God is using to speak to us, to discern the degree of implicit ownership that each stakeholder has, and to identify their ownership objectives.

Community or society at large is often viewed as the legal owner of the nonprofit organization and engages with the board and chief executive through community meetings, volunteer involvement and donor management. But if the organization's focus happens to be regional or national, then "society at large" does not function well as a stakeholder when it comes to viable engagement. Foundations and major donors came closer to being able to function as stakeholders, although laws controlling donor demand place limits on their role of being able to influence the organization through their gifts. However, having donors does provide an opportunity to dialogue with real people who have ideas about the mission and objectives of the organization. In some of the nonprofit organizations that I have served, certain customer segments also constituted a stakeholder group that were heavily vested in the success of the organization and had strong opinions about its mission and objectives (for example, the parents of children attending a day camp).

In his 2006 and 2009 books on policy governance, John Carver clarifies that not all stakeholder groups have the same role as implicit owners. Some nonprofits can identify what Carver calls "moral owners" who constitute a special class of stakeholders that provide the organization with its legitimacy and are the basis on which the board determines its accountability. These are people who might pay to be members of a membership organization such as a nonprofit automobile organization or trade association. But if a nonprofit is unable to identify a class of stakeholders as "moral owners," it is still incumbent on the organization to evaluate which stakeholder group comes closest to being what I call implicit owners.[15]

Regardless of the challenges nonprofit leaders face in identifying and engaging with them, stakeholders do keep me as a steward leader focused on fundamental truths concerning the contemporary nonprofit organization. First of all, I do not own the organization. Second, I am placed in a position of trust and stewardship to manage the nonprofit organization on behalf of the stakeholders. And third, I need to determine who the most appropriate stakeholders are and figure out a way to engage God and them to discern their objectives and goals for the organization. It's been said that the entire market economy is based on ownership and profit. A parallel for the nonprofit economy would state that the entire nonprofit economy is based on non-ownership and outcomes.

None of this presumes that the process of steward leadership will be easy or unambiguous. Engaging with stakeholders offers the steward leader the protection of collectivity to ensure the common good. That protection takes the concept of stewardship theory a step further. If a steward leader has positive managerial motivation that is driven by intrinsic desires alone (such as altruism or a sense of identification), that is commendable. But it is also easily misdirected. Steward leadership functions best when there is also an outside influence and accountability on the steward's actions that limits self-interested behavior or misdirection.

Owners, stakeholders and stewards don't necessarily think alike nor are they motivated by the same things. Significant differences can exist in perceptions, rights and goals among the three groups. Table 2 demonstrates some of these potential differences.

Table 2. Perception and values among owners, stakeholders and steward leaders

	Owners	Stakeholders	Steward Leaders
Right	Ownership, right of resource control	Influence on resource control	Management of resources
Motivation	Self-interest	Common good, personal need	Responsibility to the owners and stakeholders, altruism, fulfillment
Accountability	To the law and morality	To community or society	To owners or stakeholders
Goal	Wealth generation	Having personal needs met, society improved	Accomplishment of the owner's goals or mission
Success	Quantified by accounting	Quantified by social change	Quantified by fulfillment of the owner's goals or mission
Agency	By hired management	By board of directors and CEO	By staff
Values	Possessive	Communal	Service

The lens of ownership in steward leadership is not easy to understand or quantify, and I often struggle with other nonprofit leaders as we try to manage divine ownership, stakeholder rights and stakeholder engagement. It is a major part of nonprofit steward leadership that will always be a challenge. But lack of explicit ownership nonetheless places a weight of responsibility on the nonprofit steward leader to determine who the implicit owner or owners are and to engage them in identifying their objectives and goals for the organization.

The lens of motivation. What motivates a person to be willing to lead as a steward of resources they do not own? Why would anyone attempt to achieve objectives that come largely from others? The lens of motivation focuses on the internal intentions that drive the leader to seek, and even thrive, in this challenging triad between owner (or stakeholders), steward and organization (or resources). The heart of this second lens is best summarized in the ongoing debate between two opposing theories of managerial control: agency theory and stewardship theory. In the last twenty-five years, organizational economics and governance have been largely influenced by agency theory, which addresses managers of large corporations as agents who perform actions on behalf of the principal or owners. According to agency theory, the separation of ownership and management causes a number of challenges. Because this theory views people as motivated to maximize individual utility (in other words, to maximize personal control, wealth or authority) and minimize organizational need, managers (agents) often will not act to maximize return to owners or shareholders (principals) unless appropriate control and reward structures are implemented. Principals create these managerial incentives and controls so managers will act in the interests of the owners instead of their own.

In 1989 a new stewardship theory of governance was proposed that has been receiving growing attention. Stewardship theory states that there does not have to be an inherent problem with managerial motivation; managers can have an intrinsic desire to maximize organizational performance because of a sense of duty and identification with the owners, the organization or the organization's mission.

As an early developer of stewardship theory, Lex Donaldson in 1990 judged agency theory "a narrow model of human motivation and behavior [with] its negative moral characterization of managers and its methodological individualistic bias."[16] He proposed a positive approach to organizational economics through stewardship theory. His paper demonstrates that humans are capable of a much larger range of motives including responsibility, altruism and respect for authority, unlike agency theory's negative view of man's moral behavior.

Seven years later, Davis, Schoorman and Donaldson developed a more detailed explanation of stewardship theory. In their work these researchers describe the conditions under which both agency and stewardship theory could be necessary. They theorize that a steward's behavior is collective (focused on achieving the objectives of the organization), organizationally centered and autonomous, and it operates with high authority. The psychological factors that drive stewards are intrinsic motivation, organizational identification and the use of personal power. The situational mechanisms they identify that motivate stewards are involvement, trust, performance enhancement and collectivism.

The steward leader is driven by different internal motives than the agent leader or the owner leader.[17] Although all three types can share motives in common, overall the motivational set of the steward leader is distinctive. Stewardship theory demonstrates that steward leaders are motivated more by intrinsic and internal desires and drives (personal growth, self-actualization, achievement, affiliation) than by external rewards (wealth, authority, title, advancement). Leaders operating under stewardship theory also develop a greater sense of identification with the owners, the organization and the mission. From my own doctoral research I have found that steward leaders place a high value on altruism (unselfishness), servanthood, humility and responsibility.

We have already seen how the relationship between the owner and the steward is crucial for proper stewardship. Steward leaders do not merely know what the owner wants; they identify with the owner's aspirations and seek to fulfill them through the organization. For instance, nonprofit leaders often take on the mission of the organization as their personal mission. Steward leaders are also motivated by collaborative leadership environments instead of individualistic environments. They value the protection that plurality of oversight affords through the collaboration of owner-stakeholder, board of directors and chief executive. Therefore, the unique motivation of the steward leader drives his ability to succeed.

The lens of accountability. The third important lens of steward leadership focuses attention on the outcomes of leadership. It is defined by addressing two questions:

1. To whom is the steward leader accountable?

2. For what is the steward accountable?

The answer to the first question begins with an understanding of who the organizational owners are. If I am clear about who the owners are (whether explicit, moral or implicit), I can more readily determine the manner and content of what I am accountable for. Later we will examine how in a nonprofit organization, the board, the executive director and the staff all have stewardship responsibilities. Each of these three groups also has a different level of accountability. As I have analyzed the relationships among all three with regard to stewardship and accountability in my own research, I have concluded that the following chain of accountability in a nonprofit organization is the best way to understand each player's stewardship role:

- Staff members serve as individual stewards and are accountable to the executive director.

- The executive director serves as the understeward and is accountable to the board of directors.

- The board serves as the chief steward and is accountable to the implicit owners or stakeholders.
- Everyone is accountable to God.[18]

Is this chain of accountability to be enforced in a strict hierarchical way? Not at all, since there is an organic nature to the nonprofit organization that sometimes modifies the direction of accountability. Sometimes human accountability has to give way to divine accountability when the two conflict. Sometimes an executive director may be accountable directly to the stakeholders, but only if he or she is not put in a compromising situation of conflicting accountability between the board and the stakeholders. I do not believe, as a nonprofit executive once told me, that it is wise for the executive director to serve as "co-steward" with the board. The executive director cannot be both co-steward and accountable to the board at the same time.

Addressing the second question regarding the content of one's accountability is much more complicated. Accountability can vary based on three broad aspects:

- one's position in the chain of stewardship accountability
- the specific type of owner one is accountable to
- the owner's aspirations, desires or objectives

The first aspect of accountability, one's position in the chain of accountability, has already been briefly addressed above. The board, as the chief steward, is primarily accountable to the stakeholders to ensure that the mission is accomplished and the organization operates with fiscal responsibility (the board's duty of care, loyalty and obedience). As the understeward, the executive director is accountable to the board for the oversight and decisions that result in the accomplishment of the mission. And the staffs, as individual stewards, are accountable to the executive director for operational excellence and execution.

The second aspect of accountability is more complex. In the days of classical and biblical stewards, accountability to the owner was generally simple because there was typically only one owner. Today, our organizational structures are much more complex. We can now have large numbers of multiple owners (publicly traded companies and nonprofits), passive ownership (stockholders and paid members of a membership organization) and

HOW OUR BOARD HOLDS ITSELF
ACCOUNTABLE TO OUR STAKEHOLDERS

I've had the privilege of being associated with a Christian children's camp in the mountains of Colorado for more than fifty years. I was a camper there starting when I was eight years old, a volunteer summer staff member in my high school and college years, a counselor, speaker and a board member. Our constituency of churches and families are very faithful to the organization, often involving multiple generations down through the decades. They care deeply about the mission and ministry of the camp and want to preserve the integrity of the camp's spiritual ministry and focus on youth.

We have a number of different stakeholder groups that each have vested interest in the future of the camp. There are faithful donors consisting of former staff and campers as well as parents and grandparents of campers. The camp was started by a small group of churches that still view it as their camp and continue to support it with staff and donations. Our bylaws also stipulate a voluntary membership that is legally responsible for approving capital commitments.

With so many stakeholder groups actively involved in the camp, the board has often struggled with its accountability relationships. Sometimes we wanted to ignore the membership because we felt they didn't know as much about the reasoning and needs behind a particular capital campaign as the board did. But we learned a key lesson one year when the members turned down a capital campaign the board had approved. It turned out they were more concerned about buying the land on which we sat than putting up yet another building on leased land. They were right, and this spurred the board on to acquire the land in order to give us freedom to pursue our Christian mission without outside interference.

We always valued the churches that supported the camp, but sometimes we chafed against their involvement in electing members to the board who represented their congregation. After a series of listening meetings between the board and the leadership teams of each church, we heard loud and clear that they wanted the camp to retain its original emphasis on children and youth and not become an adult camp, which they feared was happening. Another valuable correction.

The board has seen similar benefits from pursuing a relationship and a listening posture with our donors and parents. We now pursue board members who are part of each constituent stakeholder group. We now freely share the ministry's mission, vision and strategic objectives with our stakeholders as our reflection back to them of what we are hearing. We are a work in progress as we try to annually evaluate as a board how we can proactively pursue opportunities to meet with each stakeholder group to listen and learn.

---

implicit or moral owners (nonprofit stakeholders). When there are multiple owners, the objectives of the owners need to be combined in some form through decision and governance process. For nonprofit organizations, the combined desires and objectives of stakeholders are translated into the mission, vision, values and strategies of the organization, which the steward leader pursues and is held accountable to accomplish. If there is passive ownership (with distant stockholders, members or stakeholders), the steward often knows more than the owners about the organization because he lives it every day. Even owners of classical rural farms recognized this problem. They acknowledged that their stewards needed to be given greater freedom of responsibility to make decisions based on their deeper knowledge base. The presence of implicit or moral ownership of nonprofit organizations makes accountability challenging but not impossible. When you think about it, nonprofit steward leaders probably have the greatest accountability challenge of all organizational leaders because their "owners" have all three characteristics: they are multiple, passive and implicit.

Third, and most important of all three aspects, the contemporary steward is also accountable to accomplish the aspirations, desires and objectives of the owner or owners. The steward leader may do this by maximizing the efficient use of the resources (so that the resources go further), by adding value (so that more is accomplished than the sum total of the input), by multiplying the resources (so that the organization is sustainable into the future) or by optimizing the application of resources for maximum output (so that organizational resources are used effectively). Unfortunately, many nonprofit leaders are uncomfortable with the risks associated with resource growth and leverage. But through a close relationship with God and encouragement from stakeholders, steward leaders can experience freedom to responsibly take risks by leveraging resources. This is a critical reason why steward leaders need to develop relationships with key stakeholders.

We started out this chapter by looking at Mark, a new organizational leader who knew that he was a steward making decisions and leading on behalf of the organization's members. Mark demonstrated his understanding of the lens of ownership when he frequently mentioned to his staff that neither he nor the staff "owned" the organization but merely worked on behalf of the "owners" or members. Mark was a servant at heart and was motivated by his desire to make other people and organizations look good. He also developed an organizational sense of accountability with new forms of communication he created for members, he expanded the board to represent a fuller range of the member organizations, and he developed organizational performance metrics that he was willing to publicize. His leadership caused a whole new energy of excitement and support from the members.

The Steward Leader

What characterizes the values and behaviors of steward leaders? Do they have unique characteristics, or are they indistinguishable from other leaders who follow different approaches or models of leadership (such as transformational or servant leadership)? I am not a fan of leadership-trait theory, which holds that there are traits an individual must hope to possess if he or she wants to be perceived by others as leaders. The possession of certain traits does not guarantee that a person will be a good leader any more than the absence of one or more traits automatically disqualifies one from leadership. But leadership traits are a significant part of leadership theory, and it is clear that certain traits do contribute to leadership. Therefore, we will focus on leadership characteristics to refer to the broader descriptions of principles, behaviors, values, skills and traits respective to one's leadership role.

DISTINCTIVE CHARACTERISTICS OF THE STEWARD LEADER

Only scant lists of steward leader characteristics exist in prior literature, which led me in my own doctoral research to synthesize a preliminary list from the Greco-Roman, biblical and modern sources to provide a baseline for contemporary steward leaders to confirm and refine. The following typology of steward leader characteristics is the result of that study. If a definition or description is attached to a characteristic, it comes from the detailed comments provided by my research subjects. Many of the characteristics are shared with other trait approaches to leadership, but some are clearly distinctive to steward leadership.[1] Therefore, I have placed the distinctive characteristics forward in each list and identified them as such.

Personal virtues:

- *Trustworthy and faithful* (distinctive characteristic). Steward leadership is based on relationships of trust. Trustworthiness is expressed by reliability, consistency and loyalty to stockholders and stakeholders (and to God for faith-based leaders).

- *Submissive* (distinctive characteristic). The steward leader believes that he or she must submit to the objectives and intentions of the stockholders or stakeholders. The chief executive also submits to the goals and policies of the board of directors—or must choose to leave the organization.

- *Giving, self-sacrificing* (distinctive characteristic). Steward leaders are altruistic, generous and willing to put the interests of other people and the organization ahead of their own personal interests. This, however, does not prohibit the steward from providing for his or her own needs through the organization's resources.

- *Humble.* In my research I have found that steward leaders are often uncomfortable taking credit or receiving recognition for fulfilling their responsibilities and service to the stakeholders and constituents.

- *Full of integrity.* Steward leaders define integrity as authenticity, or being the same on the outside as one is on the inside.

- *Wise.* Stewards are expected to exhibit and grow in their ability to make wise decisions.

- *Accountable, responsible.* Steward leaders accept responsibility to accomplish the mission of the organization.

- *Honest.* Steward leaders are truthful to the board of directors and other stakeholders about the actual state of the nonprofit organization, its resources and its results.

- *Transparent, vulnerable.* The steward leader is willing to share his or her thoughts, doubts and challenges in appropriate ways so that others can better guide and support him or her.

- *Loving, caring.* The steward leader sees the value in people and treats them with respect, care and concern for their welfare.

- *Hard working, diligent.* Steward leaders work hard themselves and model the kind of behavior they expect in others.

- *Visionary, purposeful.* Steward leaders believe in what they see the organization can accomplish in the future and manage toward that end.

- *Passionate.* The steward leader avidly believes in the mission of the organization.

General behaviors:

- *Maintains the identity of a steward* (distinctive characteristic). The organizational leader sees himself as a steward and leads out of that role.

- *Knows he or she does not own the resources* (distinctive characteristic). The steward leader recognizes that he or she does not own any of the resources of the organization. The steward leader is entrusted with those resources to manage for a limited period of time to achieve the owners' purposes.

- *Leverages and grows the resources* (distinctive characteristic). A very important purpose of steward leadership is to grow and multiply organizational resources through efficient use and application.

- *Recognizes levels of stewardship* (distinctive characteristic). In the nonprofit organization, steward leaders recognize that they are a part of a chain of stewardship. The board is the top-level steward, the executive director is an understeward to the board, and the staff serve as individual stewards under the executive director.

- *Serves others* (distinctive characteristic). The steward leader serves the stakeholders to achieve their goals. He or she also serves the staff and constituents of the nonprofit organization to provide for their needs and assist them in their own stewardship.

- *Accomplishes the mission.* The primary purpose of steward leadership is to manage the resources of the nonprofit organization so that the mission, vision and goals of the organization are accomplished.

- *Is able to take risks.* Risk is a normal and necessary part of stewarding resources. Some form of planning or control is necessary to responsibly manage the hazards associated with growing resources.

- *Manages material and immaterial resources.* Steward leaders manage both material resources (such as property, money and people) and immaterial resources (such as time, influence, talents and gifts).

Spiritual characteristics:

- *Strong relationship with God* (distinctive characteristic). Christian steward leaders know it is important to constantly develop their personal relationship with God (the "Lord of the resources") so they can be better stewards and leaders.

- *Motivation for steward leadership* (distinctive characteristic). The motivation for leading the Christian nonprofit as a steward is internal—as a form of spiritual obedience—and external—focusing on the future results the leader hopes will be achieved—or a combination of the two. Many Christian leaders are seeking God's ultimate approval of "Well done, good and faithful servant."

- *Called to leadership.* Many Christian nonprofit leaders feel they have a calling from God to their leadership position and to the mission of the organization.

- *Shepherd to the staff.* Christian steward leaders attempt to provide for the physical and spiritual needs of the staff and guide them in accomplishing their own stewardship responsibilities.

HOW STEWARD LEADERS LEAD, MANAGE AND SERVE

We have said that steward leadership is the efficient management and growth of organizational resources, through leading the staff and activities of the organization as a non-owning steward-servant, in order to achieve the mission according to the objectives of the owners. Inherent in this definition is the assumption that steward leaders lead, manage and serve in performing their role. The three roles are not the same, but they are also not mutually exclusive: one can lead, manage and serve at the same time. Not every manager leads, but every leader manages at one time or another and often does so without necessarily distinguishing between the two in the moment. Leadership, management and service are like three hats that the leader wears, often at the same time.

The broadest and most basic definition of leadership that I prefer is provided by Peter Northouse: "the process whereby an individual influences a group of individuals to achieve a common goal."[2] I also appreciate the distinction between management and leadership proposed by Bennis and Nanus:

> There is a profound difference between management and leadership, and both are important. "To manage" means "to bring about, to accomplish, to have charge of or responsibility for, to conduct." "Leading" is "influencing, guiding in direction, course, action, opinion." The distinction is crucial. Managers are people who do things right and leaders are people who do the right thing. The difference may be summarized as activities of vision and judgment— effectiveness versus activities of mastering routines—efficiency.[3]

Joseph Rost contends that leadership is a multidirectional influence relationship, and management is a unidirectional authority relationship.[4] The two concepts are different but not necessarily distinguished with any precision in daily activities. Leaders are often called to exercise both in the course of their responsibilities. Leadership and management are like hats (or roles) that one trades back and forth repeatedly throughout the day as interactions require.

There are many examples of classical stewards, especially in latter classical periods, who occupied high positions in society (such as governmental leaders, holders of state office and even second in line to the ruler). These stewards influenced direction, course, action and opinion (to use Bennis and Nanus's definition of leadership). Stewards in those positions motivated people toward a common vision and exercised judgment in the process. The steward of the small rural farm or local Greek business may have just been a manager, but as the size of the enterprise grew and the scope of the responsibilities increased, leadership skills were required more and more. With the complexity of modern organizations and corporations, leadership is a necessary role for most steward leaders today. Even the complex structure of the nonprofit organization, with its board of directors and executive leadership, requires leadership skills of influence, judgment, vision casting and goal setting.

The classical steward was also a manager of resources and people. These stewards were society's efficiency experts. Their owners delegated authority to them to make decisions about resource allocation and to manage the people under their care. An important aspect of how a steward manages is revealed in the contributions of Douglas McGregor (1960). According to Mc-Gregor, the assumptions managers hold about directing people within the organization determine the whole character of the organization and its management style. The key question for management is: "What are my assumptions about the most effective way to manage people?" Every managerial act rests on assumptions, hypotheses or theories, whether conscious or unconscious, and according to McGregor, typical managerial assumptions involve the necessity of control, influence or direction to get people to perform.

McGregor labels the most traditional view of managerial direction and control "Theory X," which involves three major assumptions: (1) people inherently dislike work, (2) most people must be coerced or controlled into producing adequate effort and (3) the average person prefers to be directed and wants security above all else. By following Maslow's hierarchy of needs, McGregor argues that trying to motivate people generally fails because a satisfied need is not a motivator of behavior (satisfying needs will merely produce a focus on higher-level needs that also need to be met).

However, a different set of assumptions can produce an integration of individual and organizational goals, which McGregor refers to as "Theory Y." Theory Y's primary assumptions about managing human behavior are: (1) physical and mental effort in work are as natural as play or rest, (2) people will exercise self-direction and self-control in the service of objectives to which they are committed, (3) commitment to objectives is a function of the rewards associated with their achievement, (4) people seek responsibility, (5) the capacity for imagination, ingenuity and creativity is common and (6) under the conditions of modern industrial life, the intellectual potentialities of people are only partially realized. The central principle of Theory Y management is integration, the creation of conditions such that members can achieve their own goals best by directing their efforts toward the success of the enterprise.[5] As far as I have observed, Theory Y management describes a more appropriate approach to a steward's management approach than Theory X does.

Finally, most who understand stewardship would not have any concern with associating service with stewardship. Classical stewards were invariably servants or slaves for life, no matter how high they advanced in their stewardship position. They were required to take care of the practical needs of the slaves under their control. Service was an even greater emphasis among biblical stewards (as evidenced in the parables of Jesus and the Pauline writings). And in my contemporary research on the attitudes and characteristics of steward leaders, service is frequently mentioned as a core characteristic. What is interesting to note is how many faith-based steward leaders make an important distinction between how they are called to be servants of God but that they serve people (and are not servants of their employees).

Some leaders encounter conflict when they try to combine service with leadership. For some, serving is viewed as overly self-effacing or as literal servitude. Until the advent of the servant-leadership model expounded by Robert Greenleaf, service was rarely associated with leadership. Today servant leadership is embraced as one of the top leadership models by contemporary organizational leaders. According to Greenleaf, one is a servant first and a leader second. Peter Block took Greenleaf's work and applied it directly to organizational stewardship, viewing stewardship as a more effective model for what is normally understood as leadership. According to Block, stewardship is operating in service, rather than control, of those around the leader.

In the steward leadership model, the organizational steward both serves and leads. Leadership is not subservient to service (as in Greenleaf's view) or replaced by service (as in Block's view). The steward leader leads while serving. This close association between service and leadership in the steward leader model has caused some to confuse the model with servant leadership and assume both models are the same. However, later we will compare the two and see how steward leadership, while encompassing much of what servant leadership has to offer, is more comprehensive and espouses a more balanced approach to service and leadership.

THE IDENTITY OF A STEWARD LEADER (BEING AND DOING)

The identity of the leader is not a subject that is often discussed in leadership studies. According to Peter Northouse, most leadership studies and models focus on leadership as a trait, ability, skill, behavior or relationship.[6] You can fit almost all contemporary approaches to leadership into one of these five

HOW I LEAD, MANAGE AND SERVE AS A STEWARD LEADER

Leading a nonprofit organization is not a singular role. In fact, there are a number of roles or "hats" that I wear as a nonprofit executive director at one time or another—or all that same time. Three of the most common hats that I wear are those of leader, manager and servant.

My leadership hat comes on when I need to articulate our mission, vision or values to the staff. At times I feel like a broken record because I find myself repeating over and over why we are here and where we are going. But the leadership hat is as much about focus and influence as it is about making decisions, if not more so. I try to push decision making down as much as possible to the rest of the staff, but when an unresolvable disagreement arises, it's time for the leader in me to make the call.

I've read many books on leadership that make strong distinctions between leading and managing, and they often imply that the leader should avoid getting involved in managing, as if that role diminished his or her leadership abilities. I don't believe it. As an executive director I've put on the manager hat on many occasions, if not on a daily basis, in both big and small organizations. As long as I have even a small number of key staff members who report directly to me, I need to manage. In most nonprofit organizations, the executive director has to be an "operational leader" because of the limited number of staff available to get things done. I've produced many of my own spreadsheets, typed my own letters, I have to-do lists like everyone else, and I have deadlines. In fact, I'll be honest with you—I often find comfort in spreadsheets and in the details. From what I read about the classical steward leaders, at times they were managers too because they were expected to know how to do every job on the estate or farm, even to demonstrate it if needed.

The servant's hat is another important role of the steward leader. As I learned from my studies of classical stewards, the steward never ceased to be a slave, and for good reason. When they ceased being a servant, they seemed to lose their ability to serve the master or owner as a steward. I believe in the attributes of servant leadership (which is a part of steward leadership) and in how the serving leader empowers and brings out the best in others. I've volunteered to help staff members with their responsibilities to get a job done. I've served cookies and doughnuts to the staff so they feel valued, and I've taken part in meeting after meeting with staff to help them understand their own strengths and develop a plan for where they want to go in life.

These three hats—leader, manager and servant—are the most important roles we play as steward leaders. I've worn them one at a time and in combination, but they've always been close at hand in my leadership.

---

categories, which emphasize the behaviors or activities of the leader—on doing. If you look for references to the identity—or being—of the leader, you will rarely find any mention of the concept. What the leader does, or the attributes that the leader possesses, are viewed as far more significant than who the leader is.

The servant leadership model comes closest to emphasizing the identity of the leader as a servant, although many servant-leadership writers fall short of mentioning the identity of being a servant, feeling more comfortable with the behavior of service—their doing. Greenleaf never used the word *identity*, but he did mention how "the servant leader is a servant first. . . . It begins with the natural feeling that one wants to serve, to serve first. Then conscious choice brings one to aspire to lead."[7]

Steward leadership makes the clearest case for the importance of the identity of the leader. The steward leader views himself or herself as a steward and thus leads out of that identity. When I view my identity as a steward—not an owner—I approach my responsibilities as one who is working on behalf of another, the rightful owner of the resources. There are many who have led organizations and managed people out of a sense of stewardship long before there was a leadership model by that name. If you were to ask me twenty years ago what kind of leader I was, or what leadership model I was following, I would have told you that I tried to lead like a steward. I have since found many others who feel the same way. At the time there were no books to read on steward leadership, but the identity of being a steward provided the necessary understanding for how I led differently. Being became the basis of, and foundation for, doing.

A stewardship identity is significant for leaders for a number of reasons:

- One learns how to be a servant before one understands how service influences leadership—Greenleaf's assertion is correct. In the same way, one learns how to be a steward before one can lead like a steward. Leading is a responsibility that brings its own challenges, stresses and temptations that, if not carefully controlled by a solid foundation of character and identity, can easily lead to the leader becoming self-serving and abusive.

- Everyone will be a steward of resources belonging to another at one time or another. Most employees are stewards of resources belonging to someone else. Parents are stewards of their children for a very limited time. Citizens are stewards of resources that belong to society at large. And we all are stewards of the resources of the earth that belong to God. Therefore, learning to be a steward is an opportunity available to every human being. It is much easier to lead like a steward if we have first learned how to work, parent, be a citizen or care for the earth as a steward.

- A steward leader's relationship with followers and stakeholders is defined by the steward's identity. A steward leader knows he or she must develop a relationship with stakeholders because without that relationship the leader cannot fulfill his or her obligation to fulfill the owners' goals and objectives.

STEWARDING ORGANIZATIONAL RESOURCES

We have already reviewed many of the resources that historical stewards managed, ranging from material resources to people. In the modern organization there is a wider range of potential resources the steward may be called to manage and oversee. As steward leaders mature in their understanding of their role, they often broaden the scope of the resources under their management and experience a more holistic leadership as a result. These resources go far beyond the traditional "time, talent and treasures" that many older writers on stewardship speak about. They include

- employees (talents, skills, experience, allocation of time)
- money (cash, capital, investments, debt)
- time
- a leader's own abilities
- community
- natural resources and the environment
- power and authority
- material resources (equipment, raw materials, allocations)
- an organization's history and reputation
- the organization's brand
- strategies, plans and priorities
- vision and mission
- delegation and empowerment
- our bodies and health

Again, our operating definition of steward leadership is as follows: Steward leadership is the efficient management and growth of organizational resources, through leading the staff and activities of the organization as a non-owning steward-servant, in order to achieve the mission according to the objectives of the owner. We have demonstrated how each element of this definition is important for a full understanding of this relatively new approach to organizational leadership. However, some may ask at this point, "Isn't steward leadership just a version of servant leadership? Is a completely different model really necessary?" In the next chapter we turn to those questions.

WHY I ENJOY LEADING NONPROFIT ORGANIZATIONS

I have led various types of nonprofit organizations for more than thirty years, and I love it. Leading a nonprofit challenges one with opportunities of even greater scope than those that challenge a for-profit leader. Here are some of the things I especially enjoy about nonprofits:

- Leading a nonprofit challenges you with a blend of both mission and business. Not only are you leading a missional organization that often drives the heart and soul with a greater purpose, but you are also managing a business where all of the best business disciplines apply. I've made leadership decisions that favored mission over financial benefit, but I knew that through other actions I needed to ensure that the organization was financially viable. I often reminded the staff that in the nonprofit, we had the privilege of showing what it meant to excel in both mission and good business.
- For all of the challenges that working with a board presents, when the board does its job well, you can excel as an organizational leader. The board takes the weight of stakeholder engagement, does heavy lifting in major donor appeals and leaves the executive director to focus on organizational excellence and staff development.
- I need to believe passionately in what I am doing, and by working in a nonprofit I can be part of something much bigger than profit and revenue growth. Businesses produce helpful products and services that meet human needs, but nonprofits have the opportunity to change people's lives.
- Nonprofits are predominantly rooted in a local community, which makes their services even more personal and appreciated. I like knowing that our efforts are not only valued but are changing our community for the better.

How Steward Leadership
Compares to Servant Leadership

Ralph oversees a nonprofit ministry and as long as he can remember has conceived of himself as a servant leader. When he was first introduced to the idea, he was told that this was the leadership style Jesus modeled and taught and that all godly leaders followed. Ralph tries to model servanthood in all of his interactions with his staff and clients. He believes in empowering them to use their gifts and abilities to the fullest and sees his role as a facilitator of the success of others.

Most days, servant leadership provides Ralph with the focus and spiritual basis for leadership that he appreciates, although there have been a few crises that have tested his idea of servanthood. Last year when there was an unexpected downturn in donations, Ralph was faced with the challenge of laying off a number of staff members. He didn't feel much like a servant when he was forced to let good employees go. Another time there was a major disagreement among the staff as to whether to disband a long-standing program of the ministry in order to start a new initiative. A few employees even left over the controversy, leaving Ralph to wonder how he was supposed to serve those who disagreed. But all in all he feels that servant leadership is still the best way to honor God and lead the organization.

Brian is a long-standing proponent of servant leadership as well, but he sometimes feels that he has to put the model aside when faced with certain organizational challenges that the model doesn't seem to address. When he first heard about steward leadership, he thought that it was just another name for servant leadership. But as he has learned more about it, he has realized that steward leadership better addresses issues of leadership and organizational management where servant leadership is silent. As a steward leader, he is also a servant at heart, only now he understands that he serves the stakeholders and donors of the organization in addition to his employees. In fact, when an issue comes up about changing the future mission and direction of the organization, he knows that he is primarily accountable to the board and the stakeholders for the ultimate decision, not to the employees. Brian also feels more equipped to manage resource decisions when he sees himself as a steward and not just a servant. He feels more confident in how to approach budgetary decisions, how to analyze and evaluate ministry programs, and even how to deal with the changing needs of the organization as they affect the contributions of all employees—especially long-term employees.

Ralph and Brian present real-life scenarios of the differences between the servant-leadership and steward-leadership models. In my research on the predominant leadership models applied by nonprofit executives, eight out of ten said they tried to apply the servant leadership model to their leadership. Judging from the number of books that espouse servant leadership in the for-profit sector, it is a model that has gained prominence in many other sectors as well in a relatively short period of time. The language of servanthood and service has made a permanent mark in leadership studies through prominent authors such as Robert Greenleaf, Max De Pree, Ken Blanchard, Larry Spears and Peter Block.

Is there a difference between servant leadership and steward leadership? Since a major attribute of a steward is one's willingness to serve, is the steward leadership model just a variation of servant leadership? In this chapter we will briefly survey the development of servant leadership, evaluate its basic elements and compare them to steward leadership. We will conclude by demonstrating how servant leadership is a subset of the much bigger and more comprehensive model, steward leadership.

THE HISTORY AND DEVELOPMENT OF SERVANT LEADERSHIP

Although deeply rooted in Christian heritage, the specific application of servanthood to leadership did not appear to any significant degree in business literature until 1970 with the writings of Robert Greenleaf. A

Quaker by background, Greenleaf introduced the idea of servant leadership while a manager at AT&T. The most succinct definition of this model comes from Greenleaf himself in his foundational book on the subject:

> Who is the servant-leader? The servant-leader is servant first. . . . It begins with the natural feeling that one wants to serve, to serve first. Then conscious choice brings one to aspire to lead. He is sharply different from the person who is leader first, perhaps because of the need to assuage an unusual power drive or to acquire material possessions. For such it will be a later choice to serve—after leadership is established. The leader-first and the servant-first are two extreme types. Between them there are shadings and blends that are part of the infinite variety of human nature.
>
> The difference manifests itself in the care taken by the servant-first to make sure that other people's highest priority needs are being served. The best test, and difficult to administer, is: do those served grow as persons; do they, while being served, become healthier, wiser, freer, more autonomous, more likely themselves to become servants? And, what is the effect on the least privileged in society; will he benefit, or, at least, will he not be further deprived?[1]

Seven years later Greenleaf released a compiled book of articles that expounded on the servant leader theme in different institutions: in business, education, foundations and churches. Greenleaf called for a new business ethic, encouraging organizations to strive for excellence and become greater social assets as institutions. Since people are the institution, one strives for excellence by loving the people who are gathered to render the service. According to Greenleaf, business exists as much to provide meaningful work to the employee as it does to provide a product or service to the customer. The growth of those who do the work is the primary aim of business, resulting in workers who then see to it that the customer is served. In my opinion, a major gap in Greenleaf's philosophy comes out here, when the rights and needs of owners—and the corresponding role of directors who manage on behalf of the owners—are ignored in favor of the growth of employees.

In a practical book that applied Greenleaf's concepts, Max De Pree in 1989 documented servant leadership in the Herman Miller furniture company. De Pree defines servant leadership as the process of removing obstacles that prevent others from doing their jobs and enabling followers to realize their full potential. The true leader is a listener who, within the context of his own beliefs, responds appropriately. De Pree's concept of servant leadership touches on stewardship when he says that the servant leader is a "leader-as-steward in terms of relationships: of assets and legacy, of momentum and effectiveness, of civility and values."[2] Unfortunately, De Pree doesn't develop the leader-as-steward idea any further.

Larry Spears, director of the Greenleaf Center, edited several collections of articles expanding on Greenleaf's servant leadership ideas. In his 1995 collection of essays, Spears traces the development of three major themes in Greenleaf's writings: the servant as leader, the institution as servant, and trustees as servants. He also identifies ten characteristics that are central to the development of servant leaders:

- listening intently to discern the will of a group

- striving to understand and empathize with others

- the potential to help make others whole (to "heal")

- awareness of both self and others

- reliance on persuasion rather than positional authority in making decisions

- looking at a problem from a conceptualizing perspective, thinking beyond day-to-day realities

- the ability to foresee the likely outcome of a situation

- holding in trust and being a good steward of an institution

- deep commitment to the growth of others

- seeking means to build community among those who work in an institution[3]

Few would deny the value of these ten characteristics, and many are shared with steward leaders (such as empathy, self-awareness, strategic thinking and commitment). But anyone who has led a nonprofit organization with its stakeholders and boards of directors can immediately see weaknesses in Spears's list: "the will of the group" must be subservient to the will of the owners or directors, and "persuasion" must sometimes give way to authority when one is clearly leading toward intended outcomes.

In 1998 Spears edited another book of articles around the themes of service, stewardship, spirit in the leader and servant leadership. Each article develops concepts that were only briefly introduced by Greenleaf (such as work as calling, developing trust and the leader's covenant of accountability). The section on stewardship disappoints with its cursory assent to the relationship between stewardship and servant leadership, and it fails to develop the meaning of stewardship in favor of more articles on servant leadership.

Many other books on servant leadership have followed, but several are noteworthy for their emphasis on the identity and transformation of the leader. In 2001 Jane Fryar assembled a small booklet that emphasized the importance of a leader's identity over traits and behaviors: "The essence of servant leadership springs not from a leader's traits (e.g., kindness) or behaviors (e.g., goal setting). At its heart, servant leadership is identity-based. The servant leader's core identity and core values determine his or her attitudes and actions."[4] A unique service Fryar also provided is a compilation of over fifty terms used to describe servant leaders, their values, attitudes, beliefs and approaches toward followers. Most of the behaviors and attitudes cluster around five values:

- Servant leaders place a premium on service.

- Servant leaders want each follower to live a life of significance and purpose.

- Servant leaders value the freedom and dignity of the individual.

- Servant leaders want followers fully to develop their gifts and abilities.

- Servant leaders value wholeness and growth for their followers and themselves.[5]

Blanchard and Hodges in 2002 followed with an equally small book for the Christian market on servant leadership and general leadership principles. To these writers, effective leadership starts on the inside with a transformation of the heart (character), head (beliefs and assumptions about vision, mission and values), hands (behavior or situational leadership) and habits (solitude, prayer, Bible reading, faith and accountability). The authors examine Jesus' life as an example of all these aspects of leadership and make a strong case for inner transformation as the basis for leadership among Christians.[6] A significant number of other books on servant leadership have followed since these early books, but by then the basic concepts of this leadership model were firmly established.

COMPARING SERVANT LEADERSHIP AND STEWARD LEADERSHIP

We have established that all stewards are servants, but not all servants are stewards. Therefore, servant leadership does provide a valuable foundation for steward leadership. But in and of itself, I strongly believe that as a model, servant leadership is not sufficient to address the practical issues of non-profit leadership. Let's look at a brief comparison of both models and then evaluate specific differences between the two (see table 3).

Table 3. Comparison between servant leadership and steward leadership

	Servant Leadership	Steward Leadership
Strategy	To ensure that other people's highest-priority needs are being met and they develop as persons	To achieve the objectives of the owner and stakeholders by managing people and resources for growth
Core identity	Servant	Steward
Style of leadership	Participative	Shifts between authoritarian and participative
Motivation for leadership	Intrinsic: altruism (selfless pursuit of the interests of others), service to others	Intrinsic: altruism, responsibility, respect for authority
Characteristics	Listening, empathy, healing, awareness, persuasion, conceptualization, foresight, stewardship, commitment, community	Accountability, faithfulness, submissiveness, humility, knows the "owner" (relationship), mission focus, non-ownership, self-sacrifice, risk taking
Primary action	Serve people's highest-priority needs; "servant first, leader second"	Lead the organization to accomplish the desires and objectives of the owner and stakeholders, serve the owner and stakeholder, leverage and grow the resources
Goal of leadership	Empowered followers	Fulfilled mission, sustainable organization

The role and objectives of the owner. Servant leadership does not address the role of the objectives of God, human owners, stockholders or stakeholders in how the leader makes decisions and manages others. The steward leader's relationship with the "owner" (whether explicit or implicit) is critically important and at the heart of how the leader's activities and objectives are determined.

Attitude of non-ownership. A foundational assumption on the part of the steward is that he does not own the resources that have been placed in his trust, and thus he manages them with the perspective of a non-owner. Servant leadership does not acknowledge this distinction.

Resource management. Although people are an organization's greatest resource, organizations are made up of much more than just people. In the previous chapter we saw the full range of resources a leader must manage. Only steward leadership addresses all of the resources that must be managed, the steward's relationship with those resources and the intended outcome of resource management. The servant leadership model is excellent in how it focuses the leader on the development and empowerment of employees, but steward leadership takes that foundation and extends it to all forms of resource management.

Accountability. The servant leadership model acknowledges that most leaders are accountable to others, but that fundamental concept is not unpacked with sufficient detail to assist organizational leaders in understanding their accountability lines and obligations. Many leadership studies emphasize a leader's relationship with his or her followers, but steward leadership adds an even more fundamental "following" relationship: the steward's relationship to the one he or she is following—the "owner." A leader's ability to be accountable and be a follower is at the heart of good leadership, according to Eugene Peterson:

> Leadership is . . . most basic, a way of following. And so in a culture in which there is an enormous attention to leadership, it is essential that we take a long hard look at what is previous and foundational to leadership, namely, "followership." Following enters into a way of life that is given its character and shape by the leader. . . . For those of us who are in positions of leadership—as parents, teachers, pastors, employers, physicians, lawyers, homemakers, students, farmers, writers—our following skills take priority over our leadership skills.[7]

Core identity. Almost all classical stewards were slaves or servants, yet only a small number of servants ever became stewards. The role of steward involved a lifetime of training, skill development, testing and accountability. Therefore, leading out of the identity of a steward involves greater emphasis on the leader's character, development and behavior than does leading out of the identity of a servant.

WHY I NOW EMBRACE STEWARD LEADERSHIP
INSTEAD OF SERVANT LEADERSHIP

I have been in full-time vocational Christian ministry since 1976 when I went to work for Billy Graham straight out of college. In our work it was of major importance to gain the trust of the Christian community and deal fairly with everyone involved. Our goal was to mobilize all the believers in a locality to lift up Christ in a united effort. In short, we sought to steward the resources of the involved churches and our organization toward an agreed-upon outcome; namely, to renew the church and evangelize the lost. We served God as stewards of the resources needed to accomplish this goal.

My understanding of the term *servant* never quite fit with what I understood my task to be. Serving always sounded more spiritual, but in reality what I sought to do was to lead and not to follow. The term *stewarding* referenced my objective more adequately than serving. Many times those I served needed a firm hand and a knowledgeable coach much more than they needed someone who sought to fulfill their perceived needs. We came to lead them into doing something together that they could never pull off on their own. We were serving God in doing so, but we were stewarding or "shepherding" the flock.

—**DAN S.**

Role of authority. The role of authority in leadership is rarely addressed in servant leadership literature, leading Nicholas Beadles to conclude, "A reading of the literature on servant-leadership might have one suppose that the servant-leader ought not to exercise authority or, if he does, it ought to be carefully and sparingly exercised."[8] For the steward, authority is a noteworthy aspect of her position and responsibility. The owner of the resources delegates to the steward authority as his representative to manage the resources according to the owner's desires and objectives. Steward leadership is comfortable with the concept of authority because it is not self-imposed or self-defined but delegated and limited by the owner.

Priority of service. As we have already discussed, servant leadership focuses on the leader's service to employees, who, by having their highest-priority needs met, are then empowered to meet the needs of the customer. No mention is given in servant leadership of serving the owner of the resources. The steward leader is also a servant, but the focus of the steward leader's service is first and foremost on serving the desires and objectives of the owner or stakeholders, and only secondarily on serving the needs of the employees and customers. Steward leadership doesn't deny the importance of a servant's heart but directs it toward the appropriate sources.

In my own life I have experienced personally the power and applicability of steward leadership. When I saw myself as a steward, I knew that maintaining a close and knowledgeable relationship with the board and stakeholders was crucial to my role and effectiveness. Servant leadership rarely addressed those relationships, putting its primary emphasis on my relationship with "followers" such as the employees. I continued to see myself as a servant in all relationships, but for the board and stakeholders my service came also with accountability.

As a servant leader, I enjoyed empowering and developing employees under my care, but as a steward leader I also was aware of my responsibility to meet the needs of the organization as expressed in our goals and objectives. When things were going well, both employee development and organizational needs supported one another. But occasionally I found that the particular needs of an employee did not serve the organization, and a decision had to be made. Steward leadership helped me focus on the bigger picture of the overall mission and direction, which sometimes required that an employee be encouraged to find another workplace in which to employ his or her skills and contribution.

The evaluation of nonprofit programs is a core responsibility of the steward leader. If a particular program has been a part of the organization for many years, emotions often run high when it comes time for an honest analysis of its effectiveness and strategic purpose. Stakeholders, employees, clients and even the steward leader generally all have emotional attachments to long-standing programs. When I saw myself as a servant, I felt conflicted in whose interests to best serve at the moment. When I viewed myself as a steward, I knew that the goals and objectives of the stakeholders took priority over those of the employees or even myself. That allowed me to make evaluative decisions more objectively, although still full of emotion, that served the organization the best. I remember one program in particular that I knew had to be shut down over the objection of many of the employees. It was a decision that I knew I had to make as the steward leader, but it still didn't keep me from crying most of the way home from the pain of how I knew the decision would affect some of the employees.

Steward leadership has also helped me to focus more on the strategic goals and direction of the organization while still trying to develop people. Servant leadership caused me to focus more on the development and concerns of the employees while occasionally pointing to the bigger picture. The former seemed more holistic and intentional while the latter seemed conflicted and fragmented.

Although I always tried to manage an organization so that no employee would have to be laid off, circumstances did bring me to that awful (though unavoidable) decision several times. As a servant leader, I could never justify in my own mind the conclusion that I had failed as a servant and as a leader if I had to lay people off. As a steward leader, the emotion and the pain of laying people off was still acute, but at least I knew that as a steward it was my responsibility to make the hardest resource decision of all and that such decisions were not necessarily a sign of failure.

Servant leadership is without question a predominant leadership model within nonprofit circles and is gaining popularity as a for-profit model as well. But even with its valuable emphasis on people development, it does not adequately address many nonprofit organizational issues such as non-owner leadership, resource management and growth, fiduciary responsibility, organizational management needs, trusteeship, accountability (to God or stakeholders) and the rightful place of authority and power in leadership. Many nonprofit leaders I know acknowledge that they believe in servant leadership but also admit that as a model it isn't singularly adequate to provide all of the principles necessary to explain the full range of challenges nonprofit leaders face. I certainly found that to be true in my life.

Servant leadership may share assumptions and characteristics with steward leadership, but the two are not synonymous. I have tried to demonstrate that steward leadership has greater potential to address the challenges of nonprofit leadership than servant leadership and is the more inclusive model that subsumes the

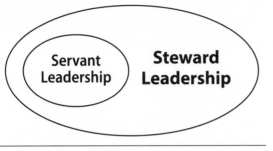

Figure 1. Servant leadership as a subset of steward leadership

other. In general, steward leadership fills in and adds to the inadequacies of the servant leader model. Therefore, servant leadership should be viewed as more of a subset within a larger and more inclusive model, steward leadership.

Stages in the Development
of Stewardship

A s the concept of stewardship progressed through ancient civiliza-tions, it developed in a way that must be understood properly in order to define stewardship today. I want to demonstrate in this chapter how stewardship progresses along definable stages that are often mirrored in the organization, specifically nonprofit organizations. During the classical period of Egyptian, Greek and Roman culture, the role of the steward and the meaning of stewardship went through four distinct stages of maturation, reaching maturity by the first century AD. We will see how these four stages mirror similar phases in contemporary stewardship in nonprofit organizations.

THE FOUR STAGES OF STEWARDSHIP

As I studied the historical steward I noticed that the first-century steward had significantly more advanced responsibilities placed on him than the steward of centuries before. It appeared that the role and expectations of the steward had undergone several broad stages of development. These stages I have called stewardship as accounting, stewardship as sustainability, stew-ardship as growth and stewardship as optimization.

Stewardship as accounting. Only a few documents exist to give us a clue as to the role and responsibilities of the steward in early Chinese, Egyptian and Greek cultures. It appears that back then stewards focused primarily on the total value of the resources and on loss prevention (which could occur through dishonesty, theft or negligence). Therefore, they maintained elaborate records of inventory levels and inflows-outflows of resources and assets. In archeological libraries from ancient Egypt, many of the fragments produced by stewards appear to be lists of resources and assets owned by their masters. On large Roman estates, stewards were required to submit their accounts on a monthly basis; these were then audited by the owner either in public (as was the case with governmental stewards or officials) or through a series of checks and balances. "Both types of audit were designed to afford a check upon 'accountability' and nothing more. It was in effect a case of examining and testing an account of stewardship."[1]

This early understanding of the steward's role involved two broad expectations: "custodianship linked with a responsibility for the prevention of theft or fraud, and secondly, the evaluation of performance."[2] The first expectation was expressed through the oversight and documentation of an accurate account of the resources subjected to audit control. This accounting was an early form of a "charge-and-discharge" statement and was in no way a statement of indebtedness, ownership or even profit.[3] The second expectation of a steward's performance was how the steward managed resources. Thus, in this first stage of stewardship, which I have called stewardship as accounting, the focus of the steward's duties is on managing (the process of overseeing the resources), accounting (an accurate assessment of the quantity and changes in resources) and authentication (or audit control).

Stewardship as sustainability. The second stage in the development of the concept of stewardship involved the introduction of operational control with the intent of resource conservation. Birnberg calls this stage "the traditional custodial period,"[4] in which the steward not only oversaw the resources but did so with the intent of "returning the corpus intact." Efficiency in the use of the resources was uppermost in importance. If the resource was a valuable gem, the steward need only keep it safe from theft in order to perform his role. However, if the resource was livestock, fruit trees or other slaves, the steward's role expanded to include providing due care and sustenance in order to ensure the ongoing state of the resource. The ultimate goal was to sustain the resource in the same or better condition than what was originally received.

In this second stage of stewardship, the steward's task is much more structured than in the previous stage and required him to possess greater knowledge and skill in how to appropriately sustain living resources. "This enhances master-servant communication, the servant's understanding of his task, the definition of data for reporting, and the ease with which the master can evaluate the servant."[5] The steward's focus is now on efficient operations (that sustain the resource), knowledge (of appropriate resource management), the duty of care, and sustainability (preserving the resource in perpetuity).

This second stage of sustainability stewardship is best illustrated by the third steward in the parable of the talents (Mt 25:14-30 and Lk 19:11-27). A master entrusts to each of three of his stewards in training a large sum of money to "put to work" in his absence. The first two stewards immediately go about investing the money in order to produce gain in the principal. The third steward, however, buries his trust in order to preserve it and return it to the master intact upon his return. The first two stewards were operating at a higher level of stewardship—they understood that growth was the objective of their master (a third stage of stewardship). But the third steward was still operating at this earlier and less mature stage of understanding, thinking that sustainability was his primary role and responsibility.

Stewardship as growth. As we just observed, by the time Jesus told his story of the parable of the talents, a third stage in the development of the concept of stewardship had arisen. In this third stage, stewards were required to play a significant role in enlarging or growing the equity of the master's resources. By this time, business and accounting systems had developed to an extent that owners were now aware of the potential for growth in their assets through reproduction, cultivation, investment or multiplication. Profit was not yet understood or measured as a business concept, but growth was.

This third stage in the development of stewardship is characterized by less specificity on the part of the master, greater judgment and freedom afforded the steward, higher risk and uncertainty, and more assessment of performance measures. Managerial control now dominates the steward's role. The steward's duties are now focused on delegated authority, on growth of assets, on uncertainty (or risk), and on goals or outcomes.

Once again, Jesus' parable of the talents reveals the development of stewardship at this third level. The instructions by the master to the stewards demonstrate that the master required a different outcome than just asset sustainability. His intent was clear in the three Greek verbs he used: "put these talents to work" (Mt 25:16), "engage in business" (Lk 19:13) and "gain by trading" (Lk 19:15). The means by which each steward accomplished these instructions was delegated to each steward as he saw fit. Based on the master's praise of the first two stewards for accomplishing growth in their talents, it is clear that they were operating at a third, more mature level of stewardship: stewardship as growth.

Stewardship as optimization. The parable of the unfruitful fig tree told by Jesus in Luke 13:6-9 gives early indications of a fourth stage of stewardship. An owner notices a fig tree that hasn't born fruit in three years and orders the steward to cut it down so that soil can be used for new fruit-bearing resources. However, the steward, confident in his delegated authority, suggests an alternative plan in which he will water and fertilize the tree for one more year. If it bears fruit as a result, the resource will be saved. If it doesn't, he will cut it down and use the ground to plant new fruit-bearing plants. The owner and steward both are operating under a form of stewardship as optimization in which resources (in this case, water, fertilizer, soil and trees) are utilized in various combinations over time to achieve optimum growth and output.

In most cases where a resource is invested, there is an optimum output from which further investments will produce diminishing returns. A tree will grow with an optimum amount of water, whereas less or more water will potentially stunt its growth. The investment of money in a business venture will produce an optimum return on investment (ROI) where the capital invested achieves its most effective and highest ROI.

In stewardship as optimization, the master entrusts assets to the steward expecting that they will be strategically managed for maximum ROI and may be converted to other applications when optimization has been achieved (or determined as unachievable). The steward operates with the highest degree of trust, independence and authority with respect to his relationship with the owner of the resources. In this fourth stage of stewardship, the steward's role is focused on effectiveness and economy, measuring and maximizing ROI, on strategic control, on flexibility (moving resources from one application to another) and on planning.

The Stages of Stewardship in Nonprofit Organizations

Even though thousands of years separate the modern steward leader from these classical examples, contemporary steward leaders often experience the same progressive stages of stewardship as they mature in their role. We can particularly observe this sequence in nonprofit organizations. These organizations may not always progress through the stages in succession, but in my experience moderate observation can often identify the stage at which an organization is being led. With a little time and the right questions, I can generally pinpoint the exact stage of stewardship maturity an organization happens to be at the moment.

Nonprofit organizations that are accounting oriented. A children's camp that I have been associated with for more than fifty years (as a camper, staff member, volunteer, speaker and board member) is a good case study of the way a nonprofit organization can progress through all four stages of stewardship maturity. The camp began in 1960 as a result of the vision of a handful of parents who wanted to create a children's camp in the Colorado mountains that put the gospel at the center of its ministry. Its first director, John, started as a volunteer who had experience in children's ministries and was also one of the principal founders of the camp. He and his wife moved to the camp and started the arduous task of renovating the older buildings on the property, which had served as a civilian conservation corps camp during the Roosevelt era before World War II. A board was formed of parents and representatives from local churches, none of whom had any experience with camping. Since John was the only one with any experience, his relationship with the board was primarily one of information and reports about progress at the camp. He had little need for oversight or decision making on the part of the board. Out of necessity he managed the camp, kept the financial books, raised money for improvements, selected volunteer counselors and determined the camp programs. It was an arrangement that lasted for years until he retired. John approached stewardship as accounting, and it fit the need of the time.

You've probably read the newsletters and brochures from nonprofit organizations that were managed by leaders with an accounting orientation. Their literature clearly stresses how many people were served, lives saved, students graduated, meals prepared or beds filled. Every last dollar spent is accounted for in great detail, and the executive director is happy to open the books to anyone who wishes to examine them. To them, stewardship is all about accurate information and reports of activities conducted. Terms that are often repeated in literature and reports are "accurate," "complete" and "accountable." When the board meets with the executive director, the agenda is full of information, facts, statistics and detailed financial reports. The board listens intently, nods and affirms that everything is in order.

There is a level of comfort in this form of stewardship, since it involves little risk, limited need for communication between board and executive director, and minimal innovation. The organization moves along like a machine, serving people, spending its budget, reaching its goals and quantifying its activities. In this type of nonprofit organization, board members often operate at one of two opposite extremes. They may be heavily involved—almost myopically so—since prescriptive direction is the form of leadership they are most comfortable with. Or the board may be virtually disengaged from involvement with the exception of attendance at board meetings.

Nonprofit organizations that are sustainability oriented. The children's camp went through several other executive directors after the retirement of the founding director, finally landing on a director who had extensive camping experience. Paul had managed several camps already and came with a clear sense of calling to the ministry and a solid commitment to the spiritual principles of the camp. He brought order and discipline to the ministry where previous directors had tried their best but didn't have his experience. The financial books were brought up to contemporary standards, formal staff training was implemented and the programs became more professional and competitive compared with the previous casual approach. Paul believed that one of the most effective ways he could develop a sustainable ministry was to mentor upcoming generations of new camp leaders, many of whom are still active in camp to this day. He had a strong sense of the camp's heritage and spoke often to the constituents about the importance of maintaining its legacy for posterity. He didn't like what he considered the "waste" of expensive building programs, so he put money into the facilities only as was necessary to maintain them. Occasionally board members questioned his "no build" policy, but he forcefully won over the majority to his way of conservatism and sustainability. He believed that his main role was to sustain camp as a legacy for generations to come.

When I interviewed a number of nonprofit executive directors, a surprising number (almost one in five) claimed that their primary role was to either "efficiently apply the resources" or "take care of the organization." These nonprofit leaders reveal a sustainability-oriented concept of stewardship. They and their boards focus on the most efficient way to use resources to ensure that those resources, and the organization, will last as long as possible. Thomas Jeavons in his book on nonprofit management profiles several organizations that are sustainability oriented: they choose simplistic cost-effective solutions over options that involve higher risk, and they are willing to forgo services whose outcomes are harder to assess over those that can be delivered in a straightforward manner. Leaders of such organizations are often concerned that the organization be sustained through their tenure and not "go down on my watch." They build systems and manage budgets with extreme care and efficiency and are proud of how much they can do with so little. To them, the ultimate goal of stewardship is sustainability and perpetuity of mission.[6]

Nonprofit organizations that are growth oriented. The children's camp in Colorado was entering its thirtieth year of ministry, and the current director had done an excellent job of solidifying the camp's programs, training, facilities and image. In one of his final acts before retiring himself, Paul hand-selected Dan as the new director, one of the younger staff members whom he had personally mentored. This new director was young, energetic, creative and fully committed to the ministry, having almost been raised at camp. And he quickly started bringing that energy and creativity to the camp's future vision, programs, growth and facilities. Dan believed that the constituents wanted camp to not only thrive but grow in how many kids it could reach each year with the gospel. He started major renovation programs on the aging buildings and drafted visions for new buildings that would add more beds and bring the facilities up to modern standards. He winterized most of the buildings so that camp could operate all year round.

With this director came a new spirit to the board that changed composition dramatically over the span of a few years. The board started dreaming about fundraising campaigns for new buildings and even personally assisted in donor calls. The constituents of supporting churches and families responded in kind, donating quickly to new campaigns and programs that were visionary and exciting. Dan's understanding of steward leadership was that he was tasked with growing the ministry, following the obvious lead of the constituents and the board.

From my observations, even fewer organizations approach stewardship as growth (about one in ten). Growth-oriented leaders and organizations often use words such as "grow," "leverage" and "multiply." They believe they have been entrusted with leadership in order to maximize the organization's outcomes through wise application and utilization of resources. To them, the output should be greater than the sum of the inputs. Money is viewed as a "nonworking resource" until it is applied through the skills and wisdom of people to provide products and services that fill a human need and change people's lives. They are not happy to merely sustain the organization: they work hard to make it grow, become more effective and do more good today than yesterday.

Organizations that are growth oriented learn to become comfortable with risk. Sometimes the risk pays off and the organization and its outcomes grow. Sometimes the risk doesn't work—which hopefully is viewed as a learning experience, not a failure. Given that resources always seem to be tight for nonprofit organizations, risk needs to be assessed carefully so as not to unduly waste resources. But when the board and the executive director are at this same stage of stewardship maturity, they are willing to put a limited amount of resources at risk for the sake of growth and development. Their boards learn how to communicate appropriate levels of risk to the leadership team. They also learn how to delegate and empower their executive directors to operate more independently. These boards focus on defining strategic goals and outcomes more than on operational directives. Executive directors of growth-oriented organizations learn how to develop multiple strategies and programs for reaching their goals. They like to test new ideas, measure and quantify outputs, and frequently evaluate outcomes.

Nonprofit organizations that are optimization oriented. Dan has now been the director of the Colorado children's camp for more than twenty-five years. A lot has changed in those years: the camp now operates all year round, it has grown its income by over eleven times, it ministers to many more campers and adults each year, and its modern facilities are becoming increasingly attractive for adult retreats. But along with this incredible growth has come refinement in the programs offered and the efficiency with which the camps are staffed. A number of traditional camping programs have been replaced with newer programs that are attracting kids where many other camps are declining. The camp operates with a stable number of full-time staff members even though it has seen triple growth in attendance. Dan has focused the staff's attention on a number of strategic objectives that are measured annually through metrics and impact measures. And the camp just completed acquisition of adjoining land that will allow it to expand its footprint for the first time in sixty years. Dan doesn't want the camp to become so big that it loses its ability to minister to each child one on one, so his emphasis of late has been on efficiency, effectiveness and impact while still managing careful growth. But the central mission of the camp still remains the same—to preach the gospel and see kids saved.

Organizations that operate at the most mature level of stewardship are optimization oriented. These organizations are the rarest of all nonprofits. Instead of focusing just on efficiency, they are equally if not more concerned with effectiveness. They understand the multiplying effect of resource utilization and further recognize that there is an optimum investment of resources that will produce the greatest outcome. They are not afraid to apply business concepts to their nonprofit mission (such as return on investment, strategy, profit or surplus, and key performance indicators). When optimum performance has been reached in a given program or service, their boards and staff are also not afraid to redirect further resources to other programs.

The boards of optimization-oriented nonprofits are generally the most diverse of all nonprofit boards, with a large percentage of business and professional skills represented. They delegate to the executive director considerable authority and independent control and focus mostly on strategy, capitalization, reinvestment in new initiatives, and forward thinking. Their executive directors often come with extensive business experience because of the need for highly developed analytical and creative skills. They are comfortable redirecting resources from programs that will probably never reach optimization to reinvest in new ventures. And they celebrate programs that have reached optimization.

WHAT IT'S LIKE RUNNING AN
OPTIMIZATION-MINDED ORGANIZATION

To run an optimization-oriented nonprofit organization takes more than desire, dedication, willpower or even thick skin. It requires a firm recognition that your organization's work is not yours, your board's or your coworkers'. It is first and foremost the work of the Holy Spirit. If your NPO's leadership and workers are not completely dependent on his leadership, moving forward in his strength and willing to risk everything to see his work accomplished, your organization will continue to be just another run-of-the-mill NPO. You might have a good story, a clearly stated mission and maybe even a good corporate reputation, but you will not be accomplishing much that can be called kingdom work.

In my experience, running an optimization-oriented, Holy Spirit–dependent NPO makes both decision making and resource allocation much easier. Why? Because each decision—whether related to efforts, personnel, time or money—requires only one basic prayer-saturated question: "What new projects or work can optimize eternal impact for the Lord and maximize return on investment?"

Unfortunately, after nearly forty years of observing leadership styles in a wide variety of both for-profit and nonprofit organizations, I can attest to the difficulty of getting an NPO to be willing to embrace even a growth-oriented path, let alone an optimization-oriented one. When such a model is verbally embraced by leadership or embarked upon for a period of time, the results are regrettably often temporary. A more or less permanent transformation in the NPO's culture is rare indeed.

I have experienced this tendency to retreat from an optimization-oriented mindset because of one of two typical reactions:

More risky ventures. If several successes are realized, the newly energized staff and subsequent increased cash flow leads to a false sense of invincibility. The organization soon replaces a disciplined, optimization-oriented approach with increasingly creative attempts to replicate these previous successes. These attempts are typified by an increase in risk, a broader spectrum of new projects or services, and a subtle shift toward focusing on increasing the size and influence of the organization. The result is usually that less-than-optimal projects are initiated and an increasing number of large-scale failures "happen." Management then retreats to the much safer confines of a sustainability-oriented or an accounting-oriented approach. The chances of these organizations ever returning to a growth-oriented focus or an optimization-oriented stewardship model are minimal at best.

Fear of losing control. A board or upper management team realizes the need to chart a different organizational path for their NPO and charges the organization's operational managers to "make it happen!" However, as soon as attempts to create significant change begin to occur, immediate reaction ensues. Changes are micromanaged or even resisted by the board or upper management—usually accompanied by pronouncements of how "responsible" they feel for every person in the organization or for the organization's reputation. In reality, it is fear of losing control, and it is played out over time by defaulting more and more to safer and more controlling approaches in decision making and giving directives. Unfortunately, many of the staff members may also join in this assault. For them, stability and safety are more important than optimization or growth.

So no one ever said running an optimization-oriented NPO was easy. But if we are aware of these typical reactions, we might be able to lead our organization through the change successfully.

—DAVE W.

In these organizations, the mission always remains central, but the means (or programs) are highly fluid. And when it has been determined that the mission has been accomplished or optimized, the organization is willing to put itself out of business or morph with a new, more entrepreneurial mission. Peter Drucker laments that there are few public-service organizations that are optimization oriented.[7] He observes how entrepreneurship and innovation are rare in nonprofit organizations and, if present, generally come from new ventures rather than existing institutions.

To summarize what we have just reviewed concerning the four stages of stewardship, table 4 lists the characteristics of each stage and how the characteristics are expressed in nonprofit organizations.

How Organizations Mature in Their Stewardship

There is no research to date that informs us how organizations and leaders develop in their understanding of stewardship, but from my observations I believe that there are a number of factors that affect the maturing process:

- No two organizations will express each stage of stewardship in quite the same way. In fact, the stages themselves are not always so distinct; they are generalized observations about a dynamic process.

- All stages of stewardship maturity can be legitimate and appropriate for a particular time and context. The more advanced stages of stewardship are not necessarily the best expression of stewardship for a young organization or new leader. For instance, in the case study of the Colorado children's camp, it was appropriate for the first camp director to function according to stewardship as accounting because that was where the organization needed to be at the moment.

- Organizations tend to express the maturity of stewardship of its leader, particularly of the executive director. The board will also adopt a particular approach to stewardship, but its approach will be more of an amalgamation of its members.

- When the board, executive director and possibly even the staff have different perceptions of their stewardship roles, they will eventually need to reconcile toward one stage of stewardship to function well together. In my experience, the stewardship maturity of the executive director seems to

Table 4. Comparative characteristics of each stage

Stage of Stewardship	Characteristics	Expressions in the Nonprofit Organization
Stewardship as Accounting	Accounting control: • Managing (over-seeing the resources) • Accounting (accurate assessment of the quantity and changes in resources) • Authentication (audit control)	• Emphasis on quantifying missional activities • Every last dollar spent is accounted for in great detail • Stress on "accurate," "complete" and "accountable" information • Board agenda full of information, facts, statistics and detailed financial reports • Little risk • Limited need for communication between board and executive director • Minimal innovation • Organization moves along like a machine (serving people, spending its budget, reaching its goals) • Board may be myopically involved in operations or disconnected
Stewardship as Sustainability	Operational control: • Efficient operations (that sustain the resource) • Knowledge (of appropriate resource management) • The duty of care • Sustainability (preserving the resource in perpetuity)	• Emphasis on "taking care of the organization" • Leaders and boards focus on the most efficient way to use resources to ensure that those resources, and the organization, will last as long as possible • Risk-averse • Willing to forgo services whose outcomes are hard to assess over those that can be delivered in a straightforward manner • Build systems and manage budgets with extreme care and efficiency • Are proud of how much they can do with so little • Ultimate goal is sustainability and perpetuity of mission

generally take precedence over the stewardship approach of the board or the staff. In the case where the board and executive director are on different stages, either the board will eventually have to accept the stewardship of the executive director or be forced to find a new executive director.

- When a new executive director joins an existing organization, it often is the case that a particular staff member or group of staff will have a different approach to stewardship than the new boss. For example, in a social service organization the case workers may be operating under a sustainability mindset (because of their focus on service delivery to individual clients), whereas the executive director may want to start serving more clients or deliver services in more effective ways. In such cases, through patience and consistent direction the executive director may be able to win the support of the staff over to the more mature expression of stewardship.

Table 4, continued.

Stage of Stewardship	Characteristics	Expressions in the Nonprofit Organization
Stewardship as Growth	Managerial control: • Delegated authority (from owner to steward) • Growth of assets through effective management • Uncertainty or risk • Goals and outcomes (as stated by the owner)	• Emphasis on "growth," "leveraging" and "multiplication" • The output must always be greater than the sum of the inputs • Work hard to do more good today than yesterday • Comfortable with risk and new ideas (interpret failure as a learning experience) • Boards communicate appropriate levels of risk with the leadership team • Boards delegate to and empower executive director to operate more independently • Focus on defining strategic goals and outcomes more than on operational directives • Develop multiple strategies and programs for reaching their goals • Measure, quantify and evaluate outcomes
Stewardship as Optimization	Strategic control: • Effectiveness and economy (measuring and maximizing return on investment) • Flexibility (moving resources from one application to another) • High degree of steward independence • Strategic planning	• Focus on efficiency and effectiveness • Recognize there is an optimum investment of resources that will produce the greatest outcome • Not afraid to apply business concepts to nonprofit mission • Willing to redirect resources when optimum performance has been reached • Boards are generally diverse (large percentage with business and professional skills) • Boards delegate to the executive director considerable authority and independent control • Boards focus mostly on strategy, capitalization, reinvestment of new initiatives and forward thinking • Executive directors often come with extensive business experience • More entrepreneurial • Mission remains central but the means (programs) are highly fluid

If not, the executive director will have to make an assessment as to whether the staff member can still function effectively in the organization.

• Not every organization will progress through all four stages of stewardship maturity. In fact, most organizations tend to eventually settle in on a particular stage in perpetuity. This may be due to the fact that organizations develop a "memory" that is hard to break or that their boards tend to find replacement directors that are similar to the previous executive director. When an organization does settle in to a particular stage of stewardship, the main issue needing assessment is whether the stakeholders are in agreement with that level of stewardship or not. If they are in agreement, then the organization may be operating at its ideal stewardship. If not, then the stakeholders would need to stimulate change in the organization through pressuring the board to change the level of stewardship or bring in a new executive director. As an example, foundations today are taking an increased role in stimulating growth and greater accountability by linking grants to specific measurements of impacts (stewardship as growth or optimization) rather than accepting previous reports of activities and expenditures (stewardship as accounting or sustainability).

- When an organization does successfully make the transition from one stage of stewardship maturity to the next, it often is stimulated by a new executive director who comes with a more mature understanding of stewardship. I have seen cases where boards have managed the change toward greater maturity, but this seems rarer than the executive director's more dominant role in the change process. The executive director seems to have a more dominant role in setting the stewardship maturity of an organization primarily because he or she lives with the staff every day and influences more decisions and actions than the board.

The role of stewards, and the resulting understanding of stewardship, has undergone significant changes since stewards first appeared in ancient history. In a similar vein, our contemporary understanding of stewardship has also undergone change as it is expressed in executive leadership and nonprofit organizations. We looked at four distinct stages in the development of stewardship that surfaced during the classical period that bear strong resemblance to four parallel expressions of stewardship in contemporary nonprofits. Each stage affects or is affected by an understanding of the roles and responsibilities of the steward leaders in the organization.

We now turn our attention to what steward leadership specifically looks like in the nonprofit organization and the three main groups of nonprofit staff: the board, the executive director or CEO, and the staff themselves. All three are stewards, but each function at different levels of accountability and resource management.

SECTION THREE

STEWARD LEADERSHIP
in the NONPROFIT
ORGANIZATION

As a leadership model, steward leadership can be applied to almost any type of organization, but the focus of this book is on the nonprofit organization (NPO), one of the most dominant and visible expressions of steward leadership today. Within the NPO, steward leadership applies beyond the role of the CEO. In fact, it helps explain the unique relationship among the three main groups of nonprofit staff: the board, the executive director/CEO and the staff themselves. All are stewards within the organization but at different levels and with different and complementary roles.

Steward Leadership in the Nonprofit Organization

P eople who have worked in a nonprofit for any amount of time sooner or later come to the point where they are baffled by the nuances of this type of organization. Why is there a board that governs the organization when the majority of the staff are far more knowledgeable about the organization and its needs? Why does a nonprofit or nongovernmental organization have so many restrictions on the activities it can pursue while a normal business does not? Why does the nonprofit sector pay such low salaries—and almost seem proud of it? What do we really mean when we say that the nonprofit organization has no owner except the community at large? Is it really healthy for NPOs to constantly have to chase donation dollars, often in direct competition with one another?

THIS STRANGE THING CALLED THE NONPROFIT ORGANIZATION

Although the history of nonprofit and nongovernmental organizations does not read along clean lines of development, certain clues are buried in the formation of their laws and organizational structures that partially explain the unique ways they function today. Charitable, educational and religious organizations have been around for thousands of years in ancient cultures and at least since colonial times in the United States. But not until the 1970s have NPOs been considered a coherent "sector" in the United States.

In early colonial America nonprofit groups were primarily known as associations. Peter Hall describes these early associations as "self-governing, with decisions made by members who often delegated power to governing boards. More importantly, they had no owners or stockholders. As public bodies, they could accept donations and bequests for charitable purposes, such as supporting education and poor relief."[1] Early in the development of charitable associations, the characteristics of non-ownership, governing boards, charitable purposes and so on were important to distinguish these organizations from business and government. I am not an expert on the development of nongovernmental organizations in other countries, but I suspect that they developed with similar characteristics.

America's founders knew that in order to protect non-ownership and social purpose, they had to create an organizational structure that was different. To do so, they borrowed liberally from earlier concepts of stewards, stewardship and holding in trust that which belongs to another. If the organization was never to be owned by any distinct person or persons other than society at large, then there needed to be governance that would hold itself accountable to society—hence, the formation of either the membership or board of directors. Board members were never allowed to consider themselves as "implicit owners." They had to function as a plurality (to avoid personal bias or manipulation), speak with one voice (to provide clarity of direction) and consider themselves "trustees" of the organization on behalf of the community (to prevent the temptation of ownership). Most of these characteristics had their roots in the steward of classical history.

Non-ownership. Stewards were rarely allowed to acquire ownership of the land or resources they managed, so their perpetual non-ownership position guaranteed a measure of objectivity and service to the owner.

Plurality of leadership. Generally there was only one steward in a classical business or estate, but that was because estates were small and there was also only one owner or master. As society became more complex and "ownership" became more diffuse (with multiple stockholders or stakeholders), the need arose for more plural oversight. The idea of plural or shared leadership dates back as far as ancient Rome and was a centerpiece of early American political thought.

Speaking with one voice. Plural leadership works only when leaders, even with their differences, are forced to speak with a singular voice and judgment.

Trusteeship. Early on association and nonprofit board members were called trustees, a synonymous term for stewards.

An equally powerful influence in the early formation of the American nonprofit sector had its roots not in classical stewardship but in political ideology. Nonprofit organizations were increasingly given greater and greater latitude of freedom and independence to operate in a manner deemed appropriate by the leadership to accomplish their mission. Traditional businesses had to pay taxes in direct support of government, but nonprofit organizations were exempt. Peter Drucker summarizes this unique level of freedom NPOs experience when he writes about "the counter-culture of the third sector":

> The nonprofit organizations of the so-called third sector . . . create a sphere of effective citizenship, . . . a sphere of personal achievement . . . in which the individual exercises influence, discharges responsibility, and makes decisions. . . . In the political culture of mainstream society, individuals, no matter how well educated, how successful, how achieving, or how wealthy, can only vote and pay taxes. They can only react, can only be passive. In the counter-culture of the third sector, they are active citizens. This may be the most important contribution of the third sector.[2]

Without question, nonprofit organizations cannot be generalized into any narrow definition of purpose, structure or type. For example, notice how the nonprofit sector in the United States is summarized by Salamon:

> The nonprofit sector is a vast and diverse assortment of organizations. It includes most of the nation's premier hospitals and universities, almost all of its orchestras and opera companies, a significant share of its theaters, all of its religious congregations, the bulk of its environmental advocacy and civil rights organizations, and huge numbers of its family service, children's service, neighborhood development, antipoverty, and community health facilities. It also includes the numerous support organizations, such as foundations and community chests, that help to generate financial assistance for these organizations, as well as the traditions of giving, volunteering, and service they help to foster.[3]

In an attempt to summarize the greatest difference between nonprofit and for-profit organizations, we have already seen how Peter Drucker focused his definition of the nonprofit on its ultimate product or objective: a changed human being.[4] And in chapter one we summarized the most germane distinguishing characteristics of the nonprofit organization:

- preoccupation with nonfinancial outcomes
- tendency toward providing a "gap" service
- different tax and legal considerations
- private sector non-ownership
- self-government
- ambiguous accountability

Given these features, nonprofit leaders quickly realize that their organizations require a unique approach to leadership that normal for-profit leadership models do not adequately address. Because the steward leader model comes from the same roots as the nonprofit organization itself, it alone best addresses these unique characteristics. In particular, we will now focus on some of the specific ways that steward leadership is expressed in the nonprofit sector. To better understand how steward leadership works in the nonprofit organization, we'll review the various levels of relationship and accountability among the primary stewards, the critical relationship between steward and stakeholder, and the relationship between steward leadership and society's recent emphasis on the triple bottom line.

STAKEHOLDERS, STEWARDS AND UNDERSTEWARDS

Steward leadership is an intimate relationship between owner and steward, between stockholder and professional steward managers, and between stakeholders and the organization's board. To visualize how these relationships work in the nonprofit organization, consider figure 2, which we introduced conceptually in chapter four.

We previously defined stakeholders as any group or individual that has an implicit claim or share in the organization's outcome by virtue of a direct contribution to or engagement in the organization. Therefore, stakeholders can potentially include donors, clients, customers, the community served and society at large. For every nonprofit organization there exists one or more stakeholder groups that are the implicit owners of the NPO. Even though stakeholders are broad-ranging groups composed of individuals who don't necessarily have singular intentions for the NPO, they still constitute the closest thing we have to a human owner who has entrusted the resources of the organization into the hands of the board and staff.

The board of directors is the chief steward of the organization's resources. Its members have been given the primary trust by the stakeholders (and typically also by law). The board has multiple members who must work together to speak and act with one voice and direction to accomplish the objectives and goals of the stakeholders, the implicit owners. As such, the board must maintain a close relationship with the stakeholders to ensure that they know what the stakeholders want and that the actions of the organization are consistent with those objectives. In the next chapter we will go into considerably more detail about how the board functions as chief steward of the organization.

The CEO or executive director is an employee of the board and thus serves as an understeward to the board. In classical times, there generally was only one steward who oversaw the affairs of a business or estate.

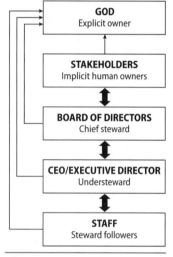

Figure 2. Relationships in the nonprofit organization

But sometimes large estates utilized a hierarchy of stewards in order to manage the larger scope of resources. In a similar way, the board serves as the chief steward, but the executive director is also a steward leader of the organization, serving at the behest of the board. The steward leadership roles of the board and executive director are complementary, overlapping and at times organic: the board's stewardship generally involves oversight, strategy, financial management and policy governance, while the executive director's stewardship involves strategy implementation, staff oversight and operational management. Boards and executive directors may share some of the above roles, step in for one another and agree to modifications of their theoretical responsibilities, all of which highlight the organic nature of their relationship. Chapter ten will examine how the executive director serves as an understeward to the board.

HOW I LEARNED TO BE AN UNDERSTEWARD BY TRUSTING THE BOARD AS CHIEF STEWARD

I was on staff in a large nonprofit for many years as a part of the senior leadership team. I wasn't the executive director, but I was a part of many team discussions as we helped the executive director set strategy and prepare for board meetings. I had a lot of respect for him as a leader and mentor, but I didn't realize I was subtly adopting his attitude toward the board.

"You have to manage the board," he said. "Don't give them too much information. And make sure you have your ducks in a row before going into board meetings so there are no surprises or changes in your strategy."

I believed him when he talked about how the board would never know as much about a particular situation as the executive director. I was to keep the board at arm's length and not let them get too involved.

Then came a shock one day when he was asked to step down and I was offered the role of executive director. I didn't feel prepared, but I knew God was leading me to accept the position. There were many surprises in my new role, but none as big as the revelation I gained from learning from the chairman of the board how to develop a genuine, trusting and collaborative relationship with the board.

The chairman had tried his best to work with the previous executive director, but he was kept mostly in the dark by the director's negative opinion of the board. The chairman believed the board was the primary body that was accountable to the stakeholders for the performance of the organization. Together, the board and executive director had separate but complementary roles in overseeing the organization, and thus they needed to respect one another's contribution to work collaboratively. Rather than viewing the board as an adversary (or an annoyance), the executive director could actually find comfort being under the protection and cover of the board.

> With trust and respect as our foundation, the chairman helped me learn how to be a true partner in stewardship. We developed board agendas together, talked openly afterward about difficult board conversations and confronted one another when we sensed either was disregarding the other's contribution. Board meetings became more strategic and focused, while staff meetings became more supportive and energized. I didn't have an understanding yet of the concepts of chief steward and understeward, but our relationship shaped what would eventually be recognized as the most effective way to work together.

Finally, in our hierarchy of stewardship the staff play a critical role as individual stewards or steward followers under the direction of the executive director. Staffs are not the servants of the executive director but rather the arms and legs of the executive director and board to accomplish the mission of the organization. Each staff member stewards his or her own special gifts, talents and experiences along with organizational resources that have been put under his or her care and management. Chapter eleven will help define more clearly how a nonprofit organization can become an organization of stewards.

THE CRITICAL RELATIONSHIP BETWEEN STEWARD AND STAKEHOLDER

For steward leadership to be fully expressed in the nonprofit organization, you will recall the three lenses by which steward leadership is characterized (which we reviewed in chapter four): the lens of ownership, motivation and accountability.

The lens of ownership focuses the steward leader's perspective on the rights and purposes of the owners of the resources, which in the case of the nonprofit are God and the stakeholders. This lens directly addresses Rodin's first level of steward relationship, which is between the steward and the stakeholders. Since a board of directors is the chief steward of the nonprofit organization, it makes sense that the board have the primary and most intimate relationship with the various stakeholder groups. The executive director will also have close relationships with stakeholders by virtue of his or her management and development function, but the executive director's relationship should never circumvent the board's efforts in continuously developing board-stakeholder relationships and communication.

The lens of motivation focuses on the internal intentions that drive the leader to seek, and even thrive, in this challenging triad of owner (or stakeholders), steward and organization (or resources). This lens clarifies the motivations that drive relationships on all four levels managed by the steward leader:

1. the relationship of the steward to the master or owner of the resources

2. the relationship of the steward to the resources themselves

3. the relationship of the steward to the recipients of the resources

4. the relationship of the steward to himself or herself

When it comes to the steward leader's relationship with the owner of the resources (level one relationship), I have found that steward leaders are strongly motivated by altruism (unselfishness), servanthood, humility and responsibility, all of which are important when serving the objectives and goals of the owner. When it comes to a steward leader's relationship with the resources themselves (level two) and the recipients of the resources (level three), the same intrinsic motivations are important since the most valuable resource in any nonprofit organization is the people. When it comes to the steward leader's relationship to himself or herself (level four), stewardship theory confirms that steward leaders are motivated by intrinsic and internal desires and motivations (such as personal growth, self-actualization, achievement and affiliation).

The third important lens that focuses steward leadership is the lens of accountability. This lens focuses attention on the outcomes of leadership and is defined by addressing two questions: To whom is the steward leader accountable? and, For what is the steward accountable? Once again, this lens is critically dependent on the relationship between steward and stakeholder, because the answers to both questions of accountability reside in that relationship:

MY STRUGGLE WITH CONTROL

It's easy for me to identify where my primary struggle lies in being a steward leader. My natural modus operandi is to be in control. As a leader and a type A personality, I am driven to be out front and to make the big decisions. I don't want to be a servant—I want to be the owner, the master. I could blame it all on the fall and on man's propensity to want to "be like God." But in reality I struggle with this because I like to be in control. So the relationship I struggle the most with as a steward leader is with the true master or owner of the resources.

With God, the ultimate owner of all, my struggle isn't overt enough for anyone to see. I wouldn't tell God directly to his face that I know better than he about how to manage his resources. My reaction is much subtler. For periods of time longer that I feel comfortable admitting, I just don't talk to him about what he wants done with his resources. I go about my day acting as though I already know what is best and doing what I want. When I catch myself acting like an owner, I generally revert back to listening prayer, but my struggle seems to return too easily.

With human owners or stakeholders, my struggle with wanting to be in control takes on more overt forms. Much to my own embarrassment, I have at times talked negatively about the stakeholders of nonprofits that I have led because I thought that I knew better than them where the organization needed to go. I've put doubt in the minds of the staff about the wisdom and experience of donors. I've given in to the thinking that, since I am more involved in the organization than the stakeholders are, I know better what the objectives and goals for the organization should be—a common mistake for stewards even in classical times who knew more than their masters but were still expected to be submissive to the owner's goals.

This struggle will probably be with me for a lifetime. But at least I know it exists and God is helping me become more aware of its existence as I mature through the years.

- To whom is the steward leader accountable in the nonprofit organization? To God and the stakeholders as the implicit owners of the resources.

- For what is the steward accountable? To achieve the goals and objectives of God and the stakeholders.

Thus, steward leadership in the nonprofit organization is dependent on a close, continuous, well-defined relationship between steward leader and owners. In chapter nine we will discuss in more detail how that relationship is cultivated and the challenges that steward leaders sometimes encounter.

Steward Leadership and the Triple Bottom Line

Lately, much has been written about measureable outcomes for nonprofit organizations. The days in which NPOs were expected simply to accomplish their mission by staying within budget and accomplishing social good are long gone. Today, more is being demanded as stakeholders become more sophisticated and organizations increasingly compete for funds. These demands are coalescing around what are referred to as measurable outcomes as defined by the "triple bottom line" (a phrase coined in 1981 for the business sector but quickly applied to the nonprofit sector as well). The triple bottom line incorporates the notion of balanced sustainability in organizational decisions. It goes beyond traditional business approaches that measure success in terms of profit, return on investment or clients served. It is a planning, accounting and evaluative approach to measuring sustainability with three dimensions: financial, social and environmental.

- *First bottom line.* Financial or economic viability (determined with metrics that measure revenue, costs, growth, return on investment and so on)

- *Second bottom line.* Social impact (metrics concern fair and beneficial business practices toward labor and the community in which an organization conducts its business)

- *Third bottom line.* Ecological or environmental management and protection (metrics track consumption, resource use and waste management)

Faith-based nonprofit organizations either add spiritual impact and change to the social bottom line or add a fourth bottom line (with metrics that measure such things as spiritual growth, conversions or key life events achieved).

The goal for any organization trying to achieve a triple bottom line is to attain balance and success in all bottom lines through the measurement and reporting of outcomes in each sphere (see fig. 3).

Among all models of leadership, steward leadership is uniquely positioned to address the triple bottom line through its emphasis on accountability, comprehensive resource management and stakeholder satisfaction. The steward leader listens intently to his stakeholders and responds by planning, developing, measuring and reporting against the outcomes that are important to stakeholders. The steward leader also recognizes and strategically plans the various resources under his control—resources that in-

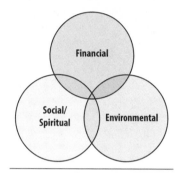

Figure 3. The triple bottom line

clude social aspects within the constituents and community being served, spiritual tools and resources, environmental resources embracing sustainability and environmental health, and financial resources. The challenge for the steward leader is to know the best way to plan, account for and create evaluative approaches to measure sustainability that fit his or her nonprofit organization. Developing meaningful social or spiritual outcome metrics is not as easy as it sounds, but it can be done with some experimentation and commitment to the process.

Steward leadership is a model that uniquely fits the nuances and needs of the nonprofit organization. We have demonstrated how nonprofit and charitable organizations developed based on stewardship concepts of trusteeship, resource management, non-ownership, stakeholders and accountability. We have also proposed a unique way of defining the relationship of stakeholder, board, executive director and staff using stewardship concepts. The relationship between stakeholder and steward leader is at the heart of how one leads the nonprofit organization, which is an aspect of NPO leadership that is virtually absent from other leadership models.

But steward leadership isn't confined to nonprofit organizations. In the epilogue we'll make a case for how steward leadership is the most appropriate model for many other sectors as well: publicly traded companies, the military, education, civil service and politics, to name just a few. But first, we'll examine what steward leadership looks like in the various leadership levels of the nonprofit organization: for the board of directors, for the CEO/executive director and for individual staff members.

The Nonprofit Board
as Steward Leader

As we have discussed in previous chapters, the nonprofit organization is an unusual construct. It was created for the purpose of ensuring the continuity and effectiveness of a mission that served the public trust. Central to that purpose is the board of directors (hereafter referred to as "the board"), which is located at the helm as the primary "trustee" of the assets and services of the organization. A useful resource document prepared by the Midwest Center for Nonprofit Leadership summarizes the primary purpose of the board:

> The board of directors of a nonprofit corporation has the ultimate responsibility and accountability for the conduct and performance of the organization. Boards regularly delegate the work of the organization to executives, staff, and volunteers, yet they cannot delegate or reassign their responsibility for that work. Nonprofit corporations are entities authorized by a state to be formed for the purpose of engaging in some form of public service, and the law requires that each such corporation must have a governing body that oversees and ultimately is legally accountable for the organization. Acting as a collective, this governing body has both the authority and the accountability for the work of the organization.[1]

DUTY OF CARE, LOYALTY AND OBEDIENCE

How does the board govern a nonprofit organization? According to modern corporate law, it does so in part by fulfilling three fundamental duties: the duty of care, the duty of loyalty and the duty of obedience. The Midwest Center for Nonprofit Leadership provides a helpful definition of each duty:

> Duty of Care, which is taking the care and exercising the judgment that any reasonable and prudent person would exhibit in the process of making informed decisions, including acting in good faith consistent with what you as a member of the board truly believe is in the best interest of the organization. The law recognizes and accepts that board members may not always be correct in their choices or decisions, but it holds them accountable for being attentive, diligent, and thoughtful in considering and acting on a policy, course of action, or other decision. Active preparation for and participation in board meetings where important decisions are to be made is an integral element of the duty of care.
>
> Duty of Loyalty, which calls upon the board and its members to consider and act in good faith to advance the interests of the organization. In other words, board members will not authorize or engage in transactions except those in which the best possible outcomes or terms for the organization can be achieved. This standard constrains a board member from participating in board discussions and decisions when they as an individual have a conflict of interest (i.e., their personal interests conflict with organizational interests, or they serve multiple organizations whose interest conflict).
>
> Duty of Obedience, which requires obedience to the organization's mission, bylaws, and policies, as well as honoring the terms and conditions of other standards of appropriate behavior such as laws, rules, and regulations.[2]

How do these fundamental duties relate to the stewardship role that a nonprofit board plays? Each has its roots in the steward-owner relationship of classical stewardship. The duty of care is essential to the role of a steward functioning in any capacity. When resources are placed under a steward's control, the owner of the resources believes that the steward will act in such a way as to advance his or her interests rather than the steward's own interests. The duty of care affirms the critical difference between agency theory (which posits that the agent will act primarily in self-interest unless controlled) and stewardship theory. The duty of care also assumes that the steward is acting in an environment of accountability for his or her actions.

The duty of loyalty is closely related to the duty of care in that the steward is once again compelled to act loyally and faithfully to advance the interests of the organization. Classical stewards were never allowed to serve more than one master; this ensured their loyalty to the master first, then to the master's resources. Regardless of a steward's personal interests or opinions, his or her first loyalty is to fulfill the goals and objectives of the owner.

The final duty involves a much-maligned term that many find offensive in today's society: obedience. With our cultural emphasis on personal freedom and independence, we cringe at the concept of being "obedient" to any other human being (unless of course we are talking about the obligations of our own children). But classical stewards were expected to be obedient to their masters by following their goals and objectives. This may have involved the occasional direct order, but by and large obedience was expressed with a high degree of independence and trust given the steward by the master, which made obedience more principled than literal. But in our modern approaches toward obedience, definitions fall short (as the definition by the Midwest Center for Nonprofit Leadership listed above does, in my opinion). Modern leaders are comfortable with the idea of obedience to organizational mission, policy and law (organizational obedience), but they are often uncomfortable with the more obvious side of obedience: the duty of obedience to the stakeholder (relational obedience). In the world of steward leadership, obedience is a necessary and important issue, and we will come back to it later in this chapter.

The Slippery Slope of "Acting Like an Owner"

As has already been discussed in previous chapters, the board stands in the position of chief steward of the nonprofit organization, having been given the fiduciary responsibility of trust by the community at large and the stakeholders.[3] And yet some boards operate under the assumption that they are the "owner" of the organization. A board may come to this belief because its members view themselves at the top of the chain of command and thus must act like owners. Alternatively, a board member may honestly believe that the best way to fulfill his or her role is to "act like an owner." In my research with nonprofit executive directors and board members, I found a surprising percentage of individuals who volunteered this philosophy of board membership. They were proud of the fact that they had come to this realization on their own as the best way to define their role as board members: "If I act like an owner and manage the resources of the organization accordingly, I will take better care of them than if I assumed the resources belonged to someone else. After all, don't we take care of our own things better than the things of others?"

There are a number of reasons why "acting like an owner" is misleading if not dangerous in the nonprofit world. In the world of agency theory, this way of thinking might be helpful. But in the altruistic world of the steward, higher values are at play and are connected with managing non-owned resources. Second of all, this way of thinking places one on a dangerous slippery slope in which "acting like an owner" today can morph into "being the owner" tomorrow. I might take better care of resources that I consider my own, but that is because I assume they are my resources, and I can do what I want with my own resources.

Finally, there is nothing to compel a board member who is "acting like an owner" to develop any relationship with the stakeholders. If I treat organizational resources as if they were my own, why would I need or want to consult with others about the goals and objectives for those resources? I become the final arbiter of resource decisions because there is no need to turn to anyone else. A board whose members believe they are the final owner of the nonprofit resources will ignore or minimize its relationship with stakeholders, viewing them at best as a funding channel and at worst as a burden.

I've served on boards that acted as though they were the owners of the organization. I don't think individual board members arrived at this conclusion out of any sense of power or control—they just felt like it made sense given their lack of understanding of their stewardship role. Someone had to make the final decisions, they reasoned as they tried to make good business and missional choices. No one told them they were accountable to anyone other than the donors, and then only as it involved management of the organization's money. They certainly didn't want donors to control the organization or its programs.

When I began to talk with the board of an international literature organization about our stewardship role as board members and our accountability to stakeholders, I was initially met with blank stares. "How do we become accountable or develop a relationship with this fuzzy group you call stakeholders? Are you saying we just let them control the organization?"

These were logical questions. Over multiple meetings we talked further about stewardship and how as board members we were not the owners but servants of the true owners, however difficult it may be to define them. Over the year the board made progress toward its stewardship role, albeit slowly. After all, everyone was having to overcome years of the dominant ownership way of thinking. We talked more and more about the different stakeholder groups and how to develop relationships with them. Board members started meeting with stakeholders, both individually and in small groups, which took a commitment since some of the key stakeholders were internationally situated. Some board members adopted a steward leader mindset quickly, while others took more time. One persisted in resisting the idea and eventually decided not to renew his term. But we started asking the question more often, "What do the stakeholders want?" and we functioned less and less like isolated owners. We were slowly becoming steward leaders instead of business leaders.

The board of a nonprofit organization needs to be crystal clear about its role as steward of the organization. They are not owners but hold in trust that which the stakeholders have placed into their responsibility. They must resist any move, however slight, toward acting like owners or dismissing the importance of their relationship with the stakeholders and the community.

Steward Leadership and Governance

Since much is said these days in nonprofit circles about board governance, it is important to demonstrate the stewardship basis for the governance role of the board as well. Governance broadly understood encompasses the decisions and actions that define an organization's mission along with its processes, policies and control mechanisms. It differs from management in that management consists of the decisions and actions that define organizational strategy. Governance is the responsibility of the board, while management is the responsibility of the executive staff. Michael Batts has written a small book called *Board Member Orientation* in which he boils governance down to the acronym SOP, which stands for strategy, oversight and policy. According to Batts, good governance involves establishing the general strategy of the organization, monitoring and evaluating the organization's activities against the mission (oversight), and establishing and refining organizational policies.[4]

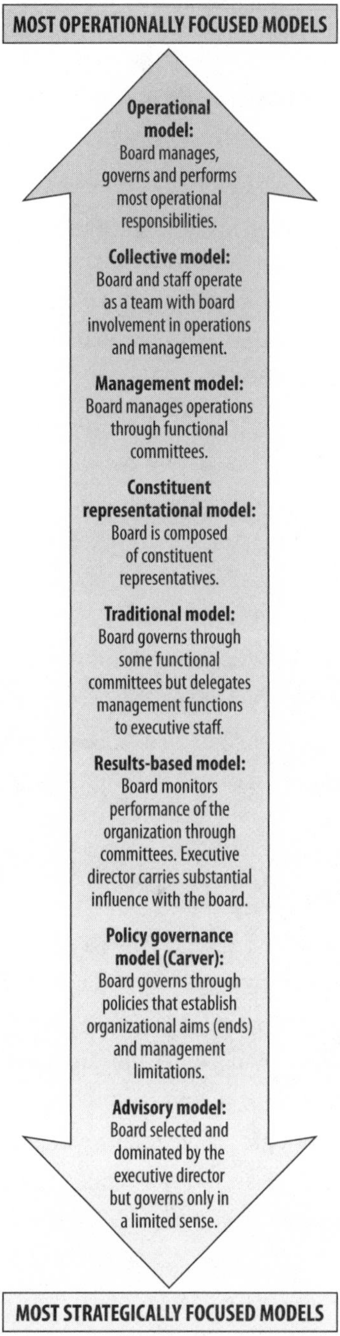

MOST OPERATIONALLY FOCUSED MODELS

Operational model:
Board manages, governs and performs most operational responsibilities.

Collective model:
Board and staff operate as a team with board involvement in operations and management.

Management model:
Board manages operations through functional committees.

Constituent representational model:
Board is composed of constituent representatives.

Traditional model:
Board governs through some functional committees but delegates management functions to executive staff.

Results-based model:
Board monitors performance of the organization through committees. Executive director carries substantial influence with the board.

Policy governance model (Carver):
Board governs through policies that establish organizational aims (ends) and management limitations.

Advisory model:
Board selected and dominated by the executive director but governs only in a limited sense.

MOST STRATEGICALLY FOCUSED MODELS

Figure 4. Spectrum of governance models

Today there are multiple approaches or models that define nonprofit governance. Mel Gil in his article "Building Effective Approaches to Governance" gives a convenient description of the various approaches to governance, which I have placed in a spectrum from most operational to most strategic (fig. 4).

In my experience, most organizations unintentionally operate within the confines of a particular model without realizing they are doing so. But one thing is true about every nonprofit that seeks to implement effective governance: behind most effective governance approaches is a foundation based on the board operating as a steward.

Governance finds its roots in the responsibilities of the classical stewards who were responsible to oversee the work being conducted on the farm, estate or business while not necessarily doing the work themselves. Although it is true that classical stewards were more managers than overseers due to the small size of the enterprises under their control, as the enterprise increased in size the need for more oversight and management layers grew as well. In the modern nonprofit organization, a strong separation between governance and management is needed. Boards function as the chief steward of the organization in order to provide a greater focus on governance, strategy and the organization's relationship with stakeholders. The board, or chief steward, is held accountable by the stakeholders primarily for the overall mission, strategy, fiduciary duties and outcomes of the organization. An executive leader within the organization is an understeward who focuses on management and operations. The executive director is held accountable for the management of operations and fidelity to the mission and policies. It's a division of labor brought about by the complicated nature of the modern nonprofit organization and the higher requirements for accountability in mission, financial credibility and outcomes. Thus, governance is an important aspect of the board's responsibility that is a specialized application of steward leadership.

THE ACCOUNTABILITY OF THE BOARD

Since accountability is one of the three principle lenses of steward leadership, it is important to define to whom the board as chief steward is accountable, and for what? We have already demonstrated that the board as steward and trustee of the organization is accountable to the explicit and implicit owners for how the organization is governed. So in general terms, the board is accountable for achieving the goals and objectives of God and the stakeholders.

A board puts itself in a position of accountability when it develops an accountable relationship with God and the stakeholders. Boards of faith-based nonprofits will often engage in certain religious activities such as prayer and Bible reading to develop their relationship with God as the primary owner of the organization. However, in my experience I have found that often these activities are either engaged in minimally (such as starting each board meeting with prayer) or the board leaves the spiritual relationship with God up to each individual member to pursue. Faith-based boards often justify this hesitancy by saying that one's spiritual relationship with God is an individualistic matter and are hesitant to push any one approach to spiritual engagement on all of its members. But as Christians and believers in God's generous desire to share his will and wisdom with us (Jas 1:5-8), shouldn't the board as chief steward lead by example seeking to continuously improve its relationship with the owner of the resources and its ability to hear from him concerning his desires and objectives for the organization? As board members, we owe that level of commitment to a growing and vibrant relationship with God.

When it comes to the board's accountability to human stakeholders, communicating about the mission, vision and values of the organization and the implementation of that mission is essential. The mission, vision and values serve in part as a double-check on the board's understanding of the goals and objectives of the stakeholders. They are the clearest articulation of the board's synthesis of the objectives of the various stakeholder groups and constituents. When the board also communicates with the stakeholders about the strategic objectives that elaborate on the mission, it is a further opportunity to expand on the board's understanding of stakeholder views: "These are the goals and objectives for the organization that summarize our understanding of what we heard from you."

As the board holds itself accountable to the mission, it additionally is accountable for other related areas:

- maintaining financial credibility and sustainability

- defining broad operational policies and processes that will guide the staff as they implement the mission and objectives

- monitoring and evaluating its own performance as well as that of the executive director

- maintaining a close relationship with the stakeholders by listening to them and communicating back to them in meaningful and simple language

The Roles of a Steward Board

There are a number of roles that a traditional board plays to fulfill its stewardship responsibility. Undergirding every one of these roles is the board's chief steward role in the organization. Even though the specific list of roles may vary depending on a board's governance model and structure, I offer the following seven roles or functions for a typical nonprofit board, each of which has a steward leadership function:

- fiduciary role

- governance role

- strategic planning role

- fund development role

- human resources role
- volunteer role
- public relations and marketing role

Let's look at each of these seven roles and how they might be expressed in a typical nonprofit organization.

Fiduciary role. This role involves the fiscal responsibility of managing the finances, legal compliance and risk of the organization through financial planning, financial processes, internal controls, analysis and reporting to government and stakeholder entities. Potential board fiduciary responsibilities might include:

- approving the annual budget
- establishing all financial policies and philosophy
- obtaining and accepting an annual review or audit of the finances
- reviewing and approving monthly financial reports
- overseeing investment policies and risks
- communicating financial information to stakeholders and legal entities to ensure compliance and accountability

Governance role. Governance is the overall leadership and guidance of the policies, decisions, processes and outcomes of the organization through the work of the staff. Potential board governance responsibilities include:

- organizing the board and its roles according to the guidelines stipulated in the bylaws
- ensuring the leadership and continuity of the board and executive director
- developing standing policies that define the "ends" or intended outcomes governing the staff's actions, decisions and processes
- evaluating the effectiveness of the board and taking action to continuously improve it
- annually evaluating the outcomes of the organization and taking action to improve them in order to meet the directives of the corporate mission, vision and values

Strategic planning role. Boards in conjunction with the executive director define the intended purpose (mission) and desired future (vision) of the organization along with its intended results (outcomes). Boards also develop and evaluate the broad means (objectives, goals, tactics) to bring that future and purpose about. Potential board strategic responsibilities include:

- establishing the mission, vision, values and outcomes of the organization
- ensuring that there are mid-term objectives (three to five years) and short-term goals and tactics (one to two years) necessary to achieve the strategic intent
- reevaluating those mid-term objectives at least every two to three years
- ensuring that there is an annual operating plan and budget
- overseeing the executive director and the staff as they operationally manage the organization to achieve that strategy through its programs and services

Fund development role. Fund development is giving leadership to the fundraising philosophy and development planning of all categories of funding (including fee for services, grants, individual contributions, special events, in-kind donations and planned giving). Potential board fund development responsibilities include:

- defining the fundraising philosophy and revenue mix strategy
- approving the annual fund raising plan
- personally being involved in fund development activities
- being regular donors to the organization

Human resources role. The board sets the values and policies that determine human resource processes, legal compliance and compensation strategies. The board has only one employee, the executive director or CEO. The executive director hires and supervises all other staff. Potential board human resource responsibilities include:

- developing the executive director's job description and annual performance evaluation process

- ensuring continued leadership and implementation of the board policies through hiring and supervising the executive director

- annually determining the executive director's compensation package (salary and benefits)

- determining and overseeing the personnel strategy of the organization (HR policies, compensation and benefits philosophy, legal compliance)

Volunteer role. Board members can govern the organization only as well as they know the organization. Volunteering to help out in the organization is one of the best ways to become familiar with its strengths, weaknesses and needs and, as a result, to govern well.

A word of caution: Board members should volunteer often, but when they do so they should remember they are wearing their "volunteer" hat and should not relate as a board member at the same time. In other words, when volunteering, act like a volunteer. Don't try to give direction to the staff or make decisions for the staff.

Public relations and marketing role. The board is the primary voice of the organization and oversees its public image, marketing messaging, public communications and pricing strategies. Potential board marketing responsibilities include:

- assisting in marketing and fundraising activities

- representing the organization to outside constituents, donors and the community

- appointing an official spokesperson for the organization

- reviewing external marketing to ensure the organization is being represented accurately and effectively

- approving all product or service pricing

When I have taught these seven roles to boards of directors, they have often become catalysts for clarity and action. A charter school board wrote board job descriptions for the first time structured around these roles. The board members of a children's ministry created an annual board review process that used the seven roles as the basis for evaluating each board member's contribution and the effectiveness of the board overall. The board of a

HOW OUR BOARD LEARNED TO VIEW STAKEHOLDERS AS OWNERS

The board of a nonprofit that I've served on for many years is by no means perfect, but we have learned, developed and grown over the years in ways that have been a great encouragement to me and others on the board. Although our engagement with the stakeholders of the organization has taken longer to realize than many other roles, I am proud of how we have taken this relationship seriously. As I look back over the years, there are a number of good things that the board has done to engage our stakeholders in meaningful ways.

1. Like most nonprofits, there are a number of different stakeholders groups with interest in the outcomes of the organization. Our board started engaging with the most influential and strategic stakeholder group first and continued engaging with them until it became a natural part of our yearly listening and communication process.

2. Engagement doesn't really get personal until you are willing to sit down face-to-face to listen and dialogue. We started like everyone else with newsletters and occasional communiqués with our stakeholders, but it wasn't until we started spending time together that real communication began. It takes many meetings to cover most of the individuals in a key stakeholder group, but it's the only way trust can be built.

3. We had to humble ourselves at times and admit that the direction we were heading was not what our stakeholders wanted. This is actually harder than you would think for a board to do!

4. When we started to engage with more stakeholder groups, we assigned specific board members to be key liaisons so there would be accountability for communication and follow-up.

5. When we heard through the grapevine that a particular stakeholder was upset about something going on in the nonprofit, we at first ignored that person, assuming the majority didn't share

the view. But over time as we gained confidence, we were more willing to lean into the disagreement and find an appropriate way to engage the disgruntled stakeholder.

6. The greatest test of our true feelings about stakeholders was the way we talked about them in board meetings. When our language was negative, or we tended to not even think about what the stakeholders wanted, our attitudes were obviously not healthy. But when we encouraged board members to share things they were learning from stakeholders and when we found ourselves asking the question, "What do you think the stakeholders want?" we knew our attitudes and relationships had taken a turn for the better.

___

social service organization used the seven roles to identify which board members were strong in specific roles to make them "champions" of that role to the entire board. They also used the roles to identify weak spots in their current board makeup so that new board members could be sought who brought strengths that were not currently represented. A private school board that used policy governance as their model used the roles to help refine the types of policies they needed to develop for the board (board policies) and the organization (ends policies).

THE RELATIONSHIP BETWEEN THE BOARD AND STAKEHOLDERS

Since a steward leader's relationship with the implicit owners or stakeholders of a nonprofit organization is so critical, a nonprofit board must work extra hard to develop and maintain that relationship. This isn't easy. It is often hard to define exactly who the stakeholders are, which stakeholders are closest to being implicit owners, and how to deal with the multiple voices and multiple directions stakeholders sometimes communicate. Although the process is fraught with challenges, when a board pursues a strong relationship with stakeholders, the results enlarge the organization's ability to focus on larger, community-driven issues. Ruth McCambridge found that when a board is internally focused (and not externally focused on the stakeholders and community), it spends the majority of its time on a "narrow focus in which [the] board's work is about organizational controls and resource development. . . . It is a pretty unimaginative and constrained approach to a situation full of need and potential."[5] McCambridge vividly illustrates this misplaced focus by profiling a nonprofit that sought foundation funds to replace its furniture while the neighborhood in which it resided was a picture of urban devastation. However, when the board is externally focused through engagement with stakeholders and constituents, its focus enlarges to the full extent of the need "out there" that the organization's mission so eloquently addresses. The board is able to put constituent interests ahead of institutional interests.

From my own experience I offer the following suggestions to help a board fulfill its obligation to develop a strong relationship with the stakeholders:

- Begin by defining who the stakeholder groups are for your organization. These can include donors, the community, constituents served, parents of constituents, specific government offices and so on. Once the potential groups are defined, it is helpful to rank them in their overall commitment to the outcomes of the organization based on "most influential" to "least influential" or "highest ownership" to "lowest ownership."

- In a few cases with special nonprofit groups there may be what John Carver calls "moral owners" among the stakeholders.[6] Moral owners are a subset of stakeholders to whom the board has a special responsibility and accountability. In a membership-based NPO the moral owners may be paid or elected members. Moral owner stakeholders always go to the top of a board's list and are generally treated with extraordinary communication and relationship.

- If multiple stakeholder groups end up ranking near the top of your list, consider "dividing and conquering" by assigning individual board members to focus on and represent specific stakeholder groups.

- Figure out ways the board can meet with stakeholder groups consistently. This may mean scheduling an annual or biannual meeting with the board as well as individual meetings with key influencers in each stakeholder group. Board members should make their attendance at such meetings a priority. Consult your bylaws to confirm if they contain any specifics as to these stakeholder or member meetings.

- Let the stakeholders know you view them as the moral or implicit owners of the organization and that you as a board are the stewards of their trust. Stakeholders may have never viewed themselves in that role before and will benefit from the clarification of your stewardship role.

- Use the mission, vision, values and strategic directions as the primary means for opening a conversation about the goals and objectives for the organization. This will give focus and specificity to your conversations with stakeholders.

- If the board hears multiple opinions from stakeholders as to the goals or objectives for the organization, it will have to consolidate and narrow the various opinions by evaluating the relative weight of each opinion and the extent that it is held by the majority.

- Remember that a stakeholder conversation is a two-way dialogue and the board has the right to express its opinion as to the purpose and direction of the organization as a means of clarifying stakeholder views.

- Don't allow the views of individual stakeholders (such as a major donor) to have undue influence over the board's final statement of the mission and objectives for the organization.

- Use communication vehicles such as periodic reports, newsletters and annual reports to provide updates and reminders to the stakeholders of the mission, objectives and outcomes of the organization.

- Publish the names and contact information of board members to the stakeholders so that they know whom to contact with questions or input.

- If the executive director develops a close relationship with a particular stakeholder, he or she should try to involve another board member in those conversations so that the stakeholder is able to develop a relationship with the board as well.

PRACTICAL ASPECTS OF A BOARD'S STEWARDSHIP

Learning how to act as a steward of a nonprofit organization is not necessarily intuitive for some people, especially leaders in a board position. It is a learned identification that takes time, encouragement and frequent reminders. I suggest that a board start by developing board documents that define its members' role and responsibilities, complete with a detailed board job description that thoroughly defines the board's stewardship role. One way to do that is to take the roles of the board previously defined in this chapter and make them a part of your board's job description and identity.

Once the documentation is complete, present steward leadership concepts and discuss them frequently in board meetings. The starting venue could be a board retreat where the group focuses on understanding their clarified role as chief steward of the organization. You may need to facilitate such a venue with an outside professional who already embraces steward leadership and can help the board through the inevitable questions that will arise. I've conducted many of these retreats and almost always find stewardship concepts embraced with enthusiasm and relief. For example: "For years I've wondered if we were missing something in our understanding of our role as a board, and now it finally all fits together." The ideal goals for such a retreat would be that the full board embrace its steward role and that the role be applied to specific board responsibilities and activities. This will result in a greater commitment to a stakeholder communication strategy, the alignment of board committees with the roles of the board, board agendas that stress stewardship and governance, and board development commitments, to name just a few specific outcomes.

The next level of application of the board's rediscovered steward leadership role will be its ongoing board meetings. A once-a-year board retreat is not enough to refocus all of a board's members on functioning like the chief steward of the organization. Old habits die slowly. So at each board meeting, members can benefit from a reminder of their stewardship role and the seven steward responsibilities. I often start board meetings by restating our role and by giving a practical encouragement on how we can be the best chief steward during our deliberations and decisions that day. Each meeting could take one of the seven roles and briefly discuss how it could be applied to the board's deliberations, decisions and actions.

Third, it always helps if one member of the board takes on the responsibility of being a steward leadership advocate for the board. The best person for this role is the chair or president of the board, but it can also be any board member who has a passion for steward leadership and is willing to remind the board of its stewardship opportunities on a regular basis. It is a completely different role than the development committee leader or development director of the organization. It is a steward leadership role, not a fundraising role.

Fourth, the revised board purpose and job description documents need to be an integral part of new board member recruitment and onboarding. Most new board members come with a variety of board experiences, some not so positive. In the recruiting process they need to hear how your board conceives of itself as chief steward and is organized around the seven steward leadership roles and governance policies. If you explain the board role in such a manner, your prospective board member will probably hear something she has never thought about before and will be able to better ascertain whether she is a right fit for the board. At a minimum you will dispel any unspoken concerns in her mind about why you want her on the board—for example, "I bet you just want me for my money, my status in the community or to fill an empty seat." Once a board prospect agrees to join the board, an onboarding process is essential to orient the new member to the specific policies, bylaws, programs and people on the board and in the organization. Every onboarding process will be different, but there are a number of resources available online (search "new board member onboarding") or in a local library to help you create your own custom onboarding process.

Finally, an important part of good steward leadership on the part of the board is to develop a strong working relationship with the executive director. If the board is the chief steward of the organization while the executive director is the understeward, both have steward leadership responsibilities. The board functions as steward over the strategy, oversight and policy of the organization and is the direct link to the stakeholders. The executive director has steward leadership responsibilities over the operations of the organization and implementation of the strategy and policies. They need to work closely together to ensure that the organization is achieving the goals and objectives of the stakeholders as defined by the mission, vision, values and strategy. Most often the board chair or president is the direct link to the executive director, and the two should meet on a regular basis to review their activities and seek to support one another. A chair should ask the executive director from time to time,

"How do you think the board is doing in fulfilling its roles?" and "What more do you need from the board that you are not getting at the moment?" Since the board and executive director share accountability to the stakeholders for accomplishment of the mission, they can also discuss how both are communicating with the stakeholders and what future visits are needed with specific key stakeholders.

Having reviewed the three key relationships that the board is responsible for (the board's relationship with itself, with the executive director and with the stakeholders), we now we turn our attention to the executive director's role as steward leader.

10

The CEO/Executive Director as Steward Leader

Howard's experience founding an international nongovernmental organization gives us a glimpse into the challenges facing executive directors who want to be steward leaders today:

I am the founder and an original board member of the non-profit where I currently serve as the executive director. From the start we wanted to infuse stewardship into the DNA of the organization. As one of those measures, we began to write a board governance policy informed by principles of steward leadership. Our board was spread around the world with members in South Korea, Nigeria and the United States, so our meetings were conducted through group email exchanges.

As the conversations took place, I quickly realized each of us had a different and unique understanding of what stewardship meant. I also realized that several of the board members understood steward leadership through the lens of a servant leader model. As the founder, I had been dominating the board, not allowing the other members to work out and internalize steward leadership for themselves. So in order for the board to mature as stewards, I needed to transition into the role of executive director and let them be the chief stewards. My departure from the board of directors now enables me to more naturally interact with the board as we all learn the intricacies of living and leading as stewards of Christ.

The frenetic pace we all seem to be living poses its own set of challenges as we have tried to mature as stewards. It takes a great deal of patience and follow-up to ensure each leader in our organization is slowing down enough to take the precious and necessary time to pray, read and learn. This is especially true when I ask our board members to read an article or a book on stewardship. Sometimes the challenge becomes overwhelming to me. I become discouraged, yet I have found when we do take the time, slow down and expose ourselves to messages on stewarding, the Holy Spirit engages us and we mature in our faithfulness to Christ.[1]

CEO, STEWARD OR UNDERSTEWARD?

Almost all nonprofit organizations recognize a CEO, president or executive director at the head of the staff organizational chart. This individual, whom we'll call the executive director, is tasked with the responsibility to manage and lead the daily activities of the organization and to execute its mission, vision, values, policies and strategy. As such, he or she is closest thing we have in today's nonprofit organization to the classic role of steward. The executive director never owns any part of the organization and yet is responsible for the management and leadership of all of the organization's resources. The executive director reports to the members of the board (who are sometimes distinguished in nonprofit literature from the executive director by being referred to as non-executive directors). Since the board is the chief steward of the organization, the executive director is an understeward in that she reports to the board and derives her strategy and directions from the board. Even if the executive director has a seat on the board, her role is different from that of other board members, and thus she will always be accountable to the board.

THE RELATIONSHIP BETWEEN THE
EXECUTIVE DIRECTOR AND BOARD

The executive director is in a very complicated leadership position by virtue of the factors that surround his role and responsibilities. As we have previously discussed, the board has only one employee, the executive director. The board manages the executive director, not through micromanagement but through strategy, oversight and policy. Thus when it comes to the communication between executive director and board, executive directors primarily focus on the measurement and outcomes of their management through high-level board reports supplemented with financial and performance data. They do not communicate everything they are doing with the board. Using John Carver's language of policy governance, the board focuses on ends while the executive director focuses on means.[2] When the executive director meets with the board, it's a type of strategic dance in which the executive director shares high-level ends information while the board focuses on strategy and avoids delving into means (operations) issues. In keeping with the primary responsibility of a steward who is accountable for results, board meetings with the executive director are generally accountability discussions, not operational decision meetings.

This dynamic communication between executive and board is no doubt one of the more challenging aspects of their relationship. Without exception, every board I have served on has had to go through a period of adjustment during which the appropriate level of communication was worked out between board and executive. Sometimes the executive tried to cover too much information with the board, resulting in meetings that were focused on reports and numbers (with little strategic interaction). Or the executive and his staff grew resentful over the length of time given to preparing elaborate board reports that were largely ignored. Since board reports have a way of drifting over time, every board needs to have an annual discussion with its executive director about the appropriate level of communication they expect. When ideas surface about new reports or metrics, there should be a discussion about whether that new request is a temporary or one-time need or a standing report. Some boards I have chaired have developed an agenda that divides the meeting between reports/updates and strategic conversation so as to protect both aspects.

Another factor that complicates an executive director's relationship with the board is that, in almost every case, executive directors know significantly more about the organization than the board does: its inner workings, its constituents and even its stakeholders. How does one maintain a respectful and subservient relationship with a superior when they know more than their boss? This problem is not unique to steward leadership since it is experienced often in modern employer-employee relationships. Even in classical documents written by landowners to their stewards, owners recognized that their stewards were almost always more knowledgeable about the affairs of the estate or business than they were. This resulted in a number of surprising concessions given by owners to their stewards: they gave respect to stewards for their knowledge, gave them a wide latitude of freedom to make their own operational decisions, showed attentiveness to the steward's opinions about strategic decisions, and engaged in respectful dialogue that went two ways.

That is why executive directors should be part of most board discussions. They need to be present in most meetings to help inform the board. Boards that have closed sessions to which the executive director is not invited should do so as infrequently as possible and only when the issues involve the executive director herself. But the flip side of this relationship is also important. In my opinion, boards should never give the executive director a voting seat on the board. This is a confusion of roles. Executive directors should meet regularly with the board and express their opinion about board issues, but they should refrain from board votes in order to maintain their distinctive role and subservient position.

In one sense the board is hierarchically superior to the executive director, while on the other hand the board and executive director are merely dividing responsibilities along strategic and operational lines (a division of labor). But practical experience suggests that the relationship is more complex and dynamic than that. Based on research conducted by Herman and Heimovics into executive nonprofit leadership, the complex, interdependent relationship of the board and executive director can best be explained with a social constructionist model recognizing that relationships sometimes emerge based not on order and rationality but on interactions molded on contextual perceptions, needs and interests.[3] Thus, successful executive directors sometimes find themselves playing a significant role in developing and enabling their board's effective functioning. Their research concludes:

> Effective executives provide significantly more leadership to their boards. This does not mean that the effective executives ordered their boards around. Rather, as the descriptions of their behavior in the critical events showed, the effective executives took responsibility for supporting and facilitating their board's work. The effective executives value and respect their boards. As a result they see their boards as at the center of their work. Their leadership is board-centered.[4]

Thus, executive directors may at times look like they are leading the board. Since they are more familiar with the organization and its issues, their input and opinions should bear considerable weight in board meetings. Executive directors live with and manage the organization every day, so their perspective is vital to a functioning board. In one sense the board and executive director together are the steward leader of the organization. Herman and Heimovics go on to suggest a short list of executive director behaviors that characterize effective executive director-board relationships:

- facilitating interaction in board relationships
- showing consideration and respect for board members
- envisioning change and innovation for the organization with the board
- providing useful and helpful information to the board
- initiating and maintaining structure for the board
- promoting board accomplishments and productivity[5]

A way to illustrate this collaborative steward leader relationship between board and executive is with table 5, which illustrates four different states of relationship between board and executive. The four types of relationship are based on low versus high engagement of each party. The four different types of steward leadership relationships are also illustrated.[6]

Table 5. Steward leadership

BOARD ENGAGEMENT			
High	**Stewardship by fiat** • Board displaces executive • Board micromanages executive or steps in to replace	**Stewardship partnership** • Board and executive collaborate in stewarding organization • High-performance board and executive
Low	**Stewardship by default** • Neither board nor CEO steward the organization • Staff or stakeholders step in to lead	**Stewardship by proxy** • Executive displaces board • Executive steps in to compensate for low-performing board or keeps board from performing
	Low	**High**
	EXECUTIVE ENGAGEMENT	

In the upper-right quadrant, the board and executive operate as partners, respecting each other's distinctive roles and collaborating on stewarding the organization. The board and executive are both operating at a high performance level. The board is engaged and creative, it understands its chief steward role and it views the executive as a true stewardship partner.

When the there is a low-performing board and a high-performing executive (lower-right quadrant), there is stewardship by proxy. This most often occurs as a result of one of two scenarios: either the executive is forced to step in to compensate for board failure, or the board is kept at arm's length by an overbearing executive (as is sometimes the case with founder-led organizations or with dictatorial directors). Stewardship by proxy results in ineffective leadership and the stakeholders are often left in the dark, wondering whether the organization is accountable to anyone.

When the roles are reversed and the board is high-performing but the executive low-performing, there is stewardship by fiat (upper-left quadrant). In this scenario, the board replaces the executive by either stepping in and doing the executive's job (in other words, becoming operationally focused) or rendering the executive ineffective through micromanagement. The executive may be unqualified for the position, untaught, underutilized or possibly even demeaned. The organization may appear to operate effectively for a while, but eventually the board will tire of its all-consuming role and be forced to deal with the ineffective executive.

Finally, in a worst-case scenario where both board and executive are low-performing (lower-left quadrant), there is stewardship by default or neglect (assuming the organization survives at all). In this case, highly committed staff members or stakeholders may step in and temporarily run the organization, but there will be little stewardship leadership or accountability, and the organization is probably on a fast track to oblivion.

In what quadrant are you and your board functioning at the moment? What changes need to be made if you are not operating with a true steward leadership partnership? A highly engaged board accepts its steward leader role in the organization, wants to work side by side with the executive director, is flexible and isn't threatened by collaborating with the executive director in stewarding the organization well. A highly engaged executive respects the board's chief stewardship role but also knows he has considerable stewardship responsibilities himself. He wants to work in a complementary relationship with the board, contributes to helping the board develop excellent board disciplines and feels valued for his contribution.

Up to this point we've been focusing on the relationship between the executive director and the board as a whole. What type of relationship should an executive director develop with individual board members? Executive directors should know board members as individuals so they are better able to understand each one's needs and unique contribution. I have always encouraged executive directors and board members to find at least one time each year when they can get together one on one to build their relationship. But they both should be careful to ensure that such offline meetings are not decisive or considered as guidance. The board needs to operate as a single unit, and offline decisions that venture into strategy or guidance are a violation of that united front. It may surprise some to know that this advice even applies to the relationship between the board chair and the executive director. Board chairs generally should spend more time with the executive director than any other board member, but the chair and executive director should be especially vigilant that their discussions not venture into setting strategy, determining policy or making operational decisions. In those matters, the executive director needs to derive his direction from the collective board.

The executive director and the board chair do have a unique opportunity to develop a close relationship that is part mentoring, part informational, part people care and part listening. The business part of such one-on-one discussions will be more limited to issues such as clarifying board strategy, policies and decisions; discussing joint stakeholder strategies; evaluating potential new board members; and jointly discussing the next board agenda. The nonbusiness part of the chair-executive director meetings will venture into more personal and supportive issues. Here are some questions I have tried to focus on in meetings between myself as the board chair and the executive director of the organization:

- Is there anything that I need to clarify about the decisions from the last board meeting?
- How are you doing? How are you feeling?
- How can the board be more effective in guiding you?
- What new resources do you need to do your job?

- What you are you excited about that is going on in this organization? What are you discouraged about?

- What does the board need to know that will make us more effective?

- You are doing a great job.

THE RELATIONSHIP BETWEEN THE EXECUTIVE DIRECTOR AND STAKEHOLDERS

Although the board has the primary responsibility to engage with stakeholders, the executive director also engages with stakeholders by virtue of his public profile, accessibility and role. Stakeholders often want access to the executive of the organization, and they can develop a strong devotion to the organization as a result of that relationship. Therefore, the cultivation of and communication with stakeholders is a partnership between executive director and board. Specific loyalties and miscommunication may sometimes occur, but the board needs to avoid the common mistake of abdicating its stakeholder responsibility to the executive director or demanding exclusive access to stakeholders. Following are some practical suggestions on how both board and executive director can develop a vibrant and informative relationship with stakeholders:

- The foundation of an effective stakeholder relationship is a plan that defines the specific types of stakeholders, the scope of the organization's accountability to each stakeholder group, and a cultivation and communication plan for each. This is not a fundraising plan, but an accountability plan that recognizes the primacy of the owner-steward relationship. Accountability is a two-way communication, so the plan needs to address how the organization will communicate the outcomes of its mission as well as listen to the stakeholders.

- The board is best positioned to deliver the primary accountability communication to the stakeholders, often in the form of a periodic or annual report and/or annual meeting. The executive director will also engage in regular communications with stakeholders through newsletters, the website and social media updates, but these communications will be more informational in nature.

- The board and executive director should share in an ongoing strategy to schedule face-to-face meetings with key stakeholders. By dividing the responsibility for these meetings between board members and executive director, you can contact a surprising number of stakeholders and gather significant information as a result.

- The executive director and board need to share with one another what they are learning from individual stakeholder discussions. This is best accomplished as a recurring conversation in board meetings.

- When the executive director has developed a relationship with a stakeholder, she needs to engage another board member in the relationship so that there are no exclusive relationships between just a stakeholder and the executive director.

THE ACCOUNTABILITY OF THE EXECUTIVE DIRECTOR

In the human realm, the executive director is accountable to the board, and the board is accountable to the stakeholders and moral owners. What the executive director is accountable for is largely dependent on the level of stewardship maturity the board and executive director are operating under (see chapter seven). If they are operating with a sustainability stewardship, then the executive director will be held accountable for efficient use of resources, sustainability and the duty of care. If the board operates under an optimization stewardship, the executive director will be held to much higher standards such as economic effectiveness, return on investment, and strategic control. Regardless of the stewardship maturity of the board, the executive director must account for executing the mission, vision, strategic objectives and goals defined by the board. The board accounts to the stakeholders for the outcomes of the organization, how well the mission is being accomplished, and how well the organization operates with fiduciary and fiscal responsibility (the board's duty of care, loyalty and obedience).

But executive directors often want more specific direction and accountability standards. They often ask two questions: "How is my performance going to be evaluated?" and "How much does the board want to know about what I/we are doing?" The first is an accountability question, while the second is a communication question. They are different but related questions. The first gets to the heart of accountability and deserves a detailed answer from the board. It is best addressed through a comprehensive section in the executive director's job description called "accountability standards" or "performance criteria." This section lays out specific criteria that are measurable, focus on ends more than means, and serve as the basis of the board's performance evaluation. With clear written performance criteria, the executive director is reminded at all times of the standards by which he will be held accountable. With clear accountability standards in hand, he will probably experience more frequent performance evaluations and will worry less about being evaluated against unstated expectations (which is a common complaint of executive directors who have no written criteria).

The second question about how much to communicate gets to the heart of what executive directors are expected to report at board meetings. Because of the dynamic relationship between the board and executive director, there is no "standard" way executive directors formulate their reports to the board. At a minimum, executive directors need to report on the progress of the organization toward achieving the strategic objectives and goals laid out by the board along with accurate financial information. But because board members are not as involved in the organization as the executive director, they often want more information about the status of programs, resource challenges, personnel issues and so on. The important thing to remember is that such reports are informational in nature and should not result in prescriptive action or micromanaging on the part of the board. Executive directors need to be responsive to their boards' communication needs (within reason) and avoid the tendency to manipulate the board with extreme communications. I've served on boards with executive directors whose philosophy was "I tell my board as little as possible so they will stay out of my way" or "I inundate the board with information so they won't have time to ask questions." Neither philosophy develops healthy board-executive partnerships.

SPECIAL CHALLENGES IN EXECUTIVE STEWARDSHIP

Because of the unique nature of the nonprofit organization, executive leaders are faced with unusual challenges as they try to lead as stewards, particularly in the areas of personnel management, entrepreneurism, risk and financial management. Since NPOs are highly concentrated in the service sector, they tend to be labor-intensive, making the executive's role in recruitment and personnel management especially important. We previously indicated that in the nonprofit sector there are constraints on a leader's ability to recruit personnel and to implement compensation systems that reward performance. This is due to a number of factors: historically lower levels of compensation when compared to for-profit positions, the lack of apparent career paths in many nonprofit positions, the dependence on volunteers to fill many staff responsibilities and the restrictive funding structure of NPOs.

So how do these factors affect the steward leader's ability to lead well? Stewards are ultimately responsible for resource management, which includes the most significant resource, people. Anything that takes control away from the steward leader complicates his job of management. Nanus and Dobbs consider personnel management a key challenge facing nonprofit leaders:

> Unlike work in the public and private sectors, much of the work of nonprofits gets done by people who are unpaid activists giving of themselves to achieve social purposes. . . . Even paid staff members often consider their salaries secondary to the psychic income they derive from helping others less fortunate than themselves. . . . Leading these kinds of people requires much more reliance on inspiration, passion, coaxing, persuasion, and peer pressure than upon authority, financial incentives, or fancy job titles.[7]

Another special challenge for nonprofit executive directors is participative decision making, which tends to be more common in nonprofit organizations than for-profit companies. For the steward leader who is trying to fulfill her responsibilities in achieving defined ends and outcomes, the participative environment makes it more challenging to influence the rest of the staff toward the goals she will be held accountable to. Steward leadership does not necessarily require participative leadership to be effective. It may be more prevalent in nonprofits because of their generally smaller size instead of any particular participative style demanded by steward leadership. A steward leader still leads with authority and is accountable to meet organizational goals and outcomes. In my experience, nonprofit staff are highly motivated by the mission and objectives of the organization, but many of them also want a greater degree of involvement in setting the goals and outcomes (or at least they want to verbalize their opinions of such). The steward leader listens to the staff, dialogues with them about the strategic directions given by the board, and works toward understanding and adoption. But if an individual member strongly believes the organization should be heading in a different direction, then the leader needs to deal with the situation in one of several ways: give that person limited time to come around, put the employee in a noncritical function of service delivery, or discuss a more suitable organization where he or she would fit.

How entrepreneurial can a nonprofit executive be? In a business, the financial liabilities of entrepreneurial activities are supported by either personal investment or institutional capital. The risks associated with entrepreneurism are personally controlled by the business entrepreneur, leaving him or her in greater control over their destiny. Peter Drucker in his book *Innovation and Entrepreneurship* decries the fact that he finds little entrepreneurism in nonprofit organizations, which he claims is permanently holding the sector back from its most effective performance.[8] In chapter seven we demonstrated that as the maturity and confidence of the steward leader develops, he is generally given more freedom to become entrepreneurial in growing and optimizing resources. But NPOs know that banks are generally reluctant to finance nonprofit entrepreneurial activity, leaving nonprofit executives to fund new ventures out of operating capital or designated funds raised from donors. Such sources of funding often come with restrictions in activity or in the overall amount of available capital. According to Dennis Young, "An internal regime of shared power and influence over policy decisions in the nonprofit organization seems to impose special restraints on the nonprofit entrepreneur. . . . This internal participative regime, which loosens the administrative control of the executive and makes it more difficult for him to translate his intentions into action, seems distinctly more prominent in nonprofits."[9]

We have seen that in classical stewardship, risk was assumed to be a normal part of the steward's world. Growing, investing and optimizing resources come with their own inherent risk of potential failure. In business, entrepreneurs have a moderate degree of control in managing risk through intuition, performance milestones, a business plan or a combination of all three. In the nonprofit organization, the steward leader will utilize the same tools and resources as her for-profit counterparts to assess and manage risk with one exception: she is also beholden to the board and the stakeholders for defining the boundaries of acceptable risk, which is a much more complicated process.

Finally, the executive steward leader is further constrained by the challenges of financial management. When for-profit budgets are put together, they are often considered guidelines that are managed with bottom-line expectations rather than line-by-line scrutiny. Most nonprofit budgets are approved and managed with myopic scrutiny. Additionally, boards often communicate the budget with stakeholders and feel pressured not to make changes even though changing circumstances may warrant it. The executive director is left with the responsibility of managing organizational finances with little freedom to modify the budget unless pursued through special board approval. Most nonprofits manage their financial record-keeping with either a bookkeeper or a volunteer, leaving them with little access to more advanced financial instruments such as cash flow projections, key financial indicators, project accounting or detailed financial reports. Except among the larger or more public nonprofit organizations, boards are typically not asking for more sophisticated financial information, and thus the challenge of executive fiscal accountability is perpetuated.

The life of the nonprofit executive steward is not consumed entirely with problems and challenges; there are many benefits and opportunities afforded the executive that facilitate effective stewardship. But nonprofit executives have their work cut out for them, and I am firmly convinced that this work is easier to understand and process when one views his or her role as a steward. It is also eased when the executive is part of a stewardship community, which is the subject of the next chapter.

We'll conclude with another story of a nonprofit leader, Matthew, who runs a multinational Christian literature distribution organization. He talks about the challenges of serving as an executive director:

> The multiplicity of roles and responsibilities is a special challenge for nonprofit leaders. In our modern climate, you are driven to measure impact and results for dollars given and report on this to donors. This is no different than the challenge facing a business leader. In addition, your service to your customers—those you are serving—needs to be done with excellence, using the

same cutting-edge leadership principles used by for-profit enterprises. Spiritual feeding, prayer and spiritual practices need to be incorporated at the personal, corporate and vision level. Finally, you need to continuously cultivate donor and partner relationships and report on significant developments to that community on a regular basis.

In a business your investors are happy if you are making their money multiply: that is often enough. Donors, in contrast, need to be fully incorporated into your mission as true partners. The modern nonprofit leader has all the pressures of business plus the need for spiritual leadership, donor relations and the financial pressure of knowing that in a human sense, serving your customers is also dependent on your ability to raise the necessary finances each and every month.

Hey, but the other side of this is that we get to live in faith, seeing God provide each and every day! That is a privilege and an honor.[10]

11

The Nonprofit Staff as Stewards

Stewardship is not just the purview of leaders or organizational executives. Our basic definition of stewardship—the management of resources belonging to another in order to achieve the owner's objectives—encompasses almost anyone who has been given resources by another to manage, sustain or develop on the owner's behalf. This certainly includes the staff and volunteers who work for a nonprofit organization. They may be stewarding a department budget, an organizational program, other people as a supervisor, or at minimum a specific role and responsibility. In classical times stewards were carefully selected individuals who had authority, but we have seen how the biblical text extended stewardship to everyone.

Becoming an Organization of Stewards

In my research of nonprofit organizational steward leaders, many shared that it was their objective to develop an organization of stewards whereby everyone viewed themselves as stewards of resources they were tasked to manage on behalf of the stakeholders, the community and God. This universal or holistic approach to stewardship was strongest in faith-based nonprofits but extended to non-faith-based NPOs as well when the leaders saw themselves as steward leaders. A steward leader's job is much easier when those around her share the same stewardship beliefs: the importance of recognizing the rights of stakeholders, the accountability that results from those rights and the freedom that comes from being motivated by a servant attitude. Rather than viewing stakeholders simply as a funding source, a source of volunteers or a source of would-be influencers, staffs can view stakeholders as legitimate partners in the mission and important allies in the definition of the organization's objectives. They learn to appreciate the strategic importance of clear mission and vision statements, values and strategic objectives as critical communication agreements between stakeholders and the organization. And they are more apt to be motivated by an attitude of service, which is integral to a steward's character and effectiveness.

Here are just a few examples of how staff members can view their roles as stewards:

- **Accountant.** "I am responsible to manage the accurate accounting of financial information and maintain clear and consistent financial processes. The resources I have been given that do not belong to me are in a sense all of the financial resources of the organization, the processes we use to manage the movement of money, and even the bookkeeper who reports to me. I am a good steward when I accurately account for the money we spend, make sure our donors receive timely and accurate acknowledgments of their gifts, and produce financial reports that are easy to interpret and tell the complete story of our activities. I consider that everything that I do directly holds us accountable to our stakeholders and to God."

- **Program manager.** "In my mind, the most important stakeholders I am accountable to are the clients we serve. I've been given incredible resources, and I know our clients depend on me to manage them well: the money that has been earmarked for this program, the other staff members who work alongside me to deliver the services, and the accurate measurement of the impact our services have on our clients. Being a good steward means delivering all of our services with a servant's heart. Sometimes I have to make hard decisions about certain aspects of our programs that are not as effective as we have anticipated, but I know that a steward sometimes has to move resources around to achieve the greatest benefit."

- **Administrative assistant.** "In my job I do a lot of tasks and don't control budgets or programs, but I work here because I want to make a difference and be known as a servant's servant. The resources for which I'm responsible aren't very visible to our stakeholders, but they make a big difference. I manage processes that keep things flowing smoothly. I'm the first person our donors and clients talk to when they call in, and my attitude and servanthood can make this the best day of their week. I serve the other staff members' needs to ensure that they can be the most effective stewards possible. In a sense, I impact almost everything we do in one way or another to accomplish our mission. That's a big stewardship!"

- *Development director.* "It's easy to understand my stewardship role. The stakeholders I focus on the most are our donors and our volunteers. I love being in this position because I have the privilege of developing individual relationships with our donors; this allows me to feel like I have direct access to their dreams and goals. They rely on me to communicate with them accurately about the impacts of our services and to respect their support decisions. In a sense, I am helping our donors become better stewards themselves of the resources God has blessed them with."

DEVELOPING STAFF WITH A STEWARD MINDSET

Unless a staff member has been raised in a church environment where universal stewardship is emphasized, they probably come to your organization with little if any understanding of what stewardship means or their role as stewards. But I have found that because of the passion many staff members bring to the mission and their values-based orientation, they are quick to embrace their stewardship role in the organization and appreciate a new perspective toward stakeholders and resource management.

Executive leadership can take a number of practical approaches to facilitate staff members adopting the mindset of stewards. It begins by embracing your own role of steward and sharing that perspective frequently with the rest of the staff: "My role here at XYZ organization is that of a steward. I don't own this organization, and neither does the board. We have been given the privilege of managing an incredible range of resources that don't belong to us but to the stakeholders, the community and ultimately to God. They trust us to manage these resources in order to achieve their goals and objectives in making a significant impact on our community's greatest needs. I am a servant of the community, a trustee of the stakeholders and a manager of someone else's property. And so are you." When you as the leader share how you view your own role, others can better visualize what stewardship looks like for them.

Take advantage of numerous opportunities to repeat these themes as you try to influence the core identity of your staff members. You want them to understand that you don't merely have stewardship duties but that at your core you view yourself as a steward, and you'd like them to see themselves as stewards as well. Create opportunities to talk with the staff about specific aspects of stewardship they may never have heard before:

- who the stakeholders are in the organization
- the important role stakeholders have in the organization
- why it's important to communicate with and listen to the stakeholders
- what stakeholders will hold you accountable for
- how as stewards we are accountable to both God and stakeholders
- the range of resources you have been given to manage
- how being a steward means both dependent and independent decision making
- how the board, executive director and staff relate to one another as stewards at different levels

Consider leading your staff through the following exercise in which every person wrestles with the meaning of stewardship and their own stewardship role in the organization:

1. Review who stewards were in history and in the Bible. Read the parable of the talents (Mt 25:14-30) and explain how each steward did or did not fulfill his stewardship responsibilities.

2. Explain the difference between owners and stakeholders. Then have a conversation with employees about who the stakeholders of your organization are. Write their answers down on a whiteboard to be visible for a later exercise. Point out that some stakeholders are more important to the organization as "moral owners" than others, and circle several you would put at the top of the list.

3. As a group, brainstorm the various resources that everyone in the organization has been asked to manage on behalf of the stakeholders. Write the list on a whiteboard for everyone to see. If you think they are missing important resources, suggest several of your own to add to the list.

4. Give the employees ten minutes to individually make a list of the resources they personally steward in their role. If people have trouble making their list, encourage them to talk with their teammates or other employees with similar positions.

5. Organize employees into groups of three or four or department groups to share their lists. Have employees read their lists out loud to the small group one by one, encouraging teammates to add additional resources to one another's lists.

6. Now direct employees to work individually again for five to ten minutes to write their own stewardship declaration by writing a short paragraph finishing the thought, "I am a steward here at XYZ organization when I . . ." To help them know what to write, read your own stewardship statement that you have prepared beforehand or refer to the stewardship statements listed previously in this chapter.

7. To conclude, ask for a few volunteers who are willing to read their personal stewardship statement. Encourage every employee to post the stewardship statement in a prominent place on his or her desk.

8. When you visit employees at their desks in the future, occasionally ask them to read their stewardship statement to you and affirm the importance of their stewardship to the organization.

Here are additional suggestions I have experienced in the nonprofit organizations I have led that have helped staff develop the mindset of a steward:

- Where possible, insert stewardship language into the job descriptions of staff members. Insert phrases such as "has the mind of a steward" in the qualifications section or "stewards X resources by . . ." in the responsibilities section of the job description.

- While explaining how all members of the organization (board, executive director and staff) are stewards together, clarify how each has different stewardship responsibilities and authority (the board as chief steward, the executive director as understeward and staff as steward followers).

- Emphasize how outcomes are far more important to stakeholders than activities, thus affecting what everyone will be held accountable for and how to best communicate with stakeholders. Staff members sometimes focus on how busy they are and on what they are doing (activities), but stakeholders care more about the outcomes of such activities.

- Educate staff on the four levels of development in the concept of stewardship (chapter seven) and where your organization falls in that spectrum. This will help set the context for future discussions about growth in resource development, program evaluation, risk, optimization and maximizing impact.

- Some staff members may need help in clarifying the resources they are responsible to manage. Even low-level employees are responsible to steward the supplies they consume; their own skills, abilities and time and even the brand and image of the organization as they interact with constituents and stakeholders.

Challenges in Developing Stewardship in Others

I have encountered several unique challenges when trying to encourage staff to serve with the mindset of stewards. One is the misconception that if I personally have resources I am responsible to steward, then I have the freedom to make decisions about those resources on my own. Some staff members may apply this misconception through a degree of independence that pits their decision-making authority against that of their supervisor or boss. It is a confusion of the dependent versus independent nature of a steward's role. All stewards, regardless of their level of authority or experience, experience both dependency on their owner or boss and a level of independence in making some decisions on their own. The key is to clarify the level of decision-making authority each staff member has over the resources he or she manages.

Another challenge in encouraging staff to see themselves as stewards is helping them understand how to relate to stakeholders. All staff members will probably encounter stakeholders in the course of their duties as they interact with donors, volunteers and constituents. When staffs understand the importance associated with seeking the input and goals of stakeholders, some may take that responsibility to mean they need to personally ask individual stakeholders their opinions about the organization's goals and objectives. As a result, they may feel pressure to either act on that input or encourage other staff members to take that input as guidance. Help staff

HOW I DEVELOPED AN ORGANIZATION
OF EMPLOYEE STEWARDS

When I first started working at NavPress Publishing, I was one of a number of staff members in the marketing department. I quickly realized how special the responsibilities we had been given were. We were managing more than 500 titles that some 350 authors had poured their lives into. We had department budgets that easily totaled in the millions and worked with many highly skilled veterans of publishing. We carried on the NavPress brand, which for more than thirty years had stood for trustworthy, biblical and practical resources. Our readers told us story after story about how their lives were permanently changed as a result of the Holy Spirit using one of our books.

It was in those early years as an employee that I began to learn what stewardship meant. I had never managed sums of money as large as I did in that job, and I never had viewed the products that we published as powerful spiritual resources until I saw the impact they had on others. I began to see myself as a steward who came to work every day, was given incredibly rich resources to manage, and was accountable for how I managed them to God first, the Navigators organization second and the authors third. Yes, I was working for a human boss to whom I was also accountable, but somehow I felt that my priorities were to the others first.

As I moved into management at NavPress, I never forgot what I had learned about stewardship as an employee, and I wanted to help others have the same excitement about being a steward. I started talking more openly about "the privilege we have here of being stewards of incredible resources." Stewardship became one of our core values as we reminded one another of who we were really working for. I spent time with every new employee orienting him or her to what it meant to live like a steward and reviewing all of the resources placed in that person's hands every day. When disagreements came up with Navigators leadership or one of our authors, we learned to approach those conversations as stewards and not as owners. One of the qualifications I looked for in new supervisors and managers was "demonstrated servanthood and steward leadership."

Trying to develop an entire organization of stewards was an ongoing challenge that was never complete. There were always the challenges of missed financial goals, underperforming book sales and human error. We would become better resource managers in some areas while others still suffered. But we always knew what our goal was: to hear, "Well done, good and faithful servant."

---

members to understand that the board is the primary body that communicates officially with stakeholders, and that such input is considered in aggregate and not individually. Encourage them not to feel like they need to engage in strategic conversations with stakeholders.

A final common challenge is the misconception that if we are using "other people's money," we should be as conservative as possible, always seek ways to save money and avoid risk. A related misconception is that nonprofits should avoid cutting back or shutting down programs. This misconception is often based on the assumption that nonprofits should continue serving all audiences, however small. Their reasoning goes as follows: "There is no doubt some customer or stakeholder out there who needs our services, and since our mission is to serve our community through these services, we need to serve them no matter how few." This misconception confirms Peter Drucker's lament concerning how the majority of nonprofit organizations are out to "maximize rather than optimize" their impact, meaning that they justify maintaining old mission emphases or programs because the need has not been met yet.[1] Staff members are intimately and passionately involved in program delivery and constituent interaction and thus can be biased toward the need for such programs. But as an organization matures in its understanding of stewardship, it learns how to become more comfortable with growth, innovation and optimization. Staff members who focus on saving money at all costs or on avoiding risk can be affirmed for their "sustainability" mindset, which is a form of stewardship, but should also be encouraged to expand their understanding into more advanced stages of stewardship. In developing a culture of stewards, your role as the executive director is to help the staff understand that the high cost of serving a few constituents may in actuality be poor stewardship and that evaluation and resource reallocation may be the best stewardship decision that can be made. Celebrate the programs that need to be diminished or shut down for the impact that they did have, then clarify how the reallocated resources can impact even more people while still staying true to the mission.

Evaluation, risk, growth and optimization should become a part of our nonprofit language and understanding of what constitutes effective stewardship, even among the staff. Developing and leading an organization of stewards is well worth the effort and will only increase our own effectiveness as steward leaders.

Epilogue

Steward Leadership for the Rest of the World

There are plenty of success stories all around us of steward leaders who understand their role and apply it with excellence. I conclude this book with a recap of just one of those steward-led organizations to show what success and "Well done" can look like. It's the children's camp in the mountains of Colorado that we've discussed from time to time. The camp has formally been in existence for fifty-five years now and is being led by its sixth executive director. Like all new organizations, it began with only a vague idea of what stewardship meant and a fledgling attempt by a board and executive director at honoring the goals and desires of the stakeholders. From the beginning the bylaws stipulated that the organization appropriately belonged to the members of the corporation, and the responsibilities and involvement of those members was clearly laid out. Anyone could be a member, and only members could approve certain decisions of the corporation—not even the board could approve those. Over the years the membership waxed and waned depending on how well the board and the staff understood and supported their role, but as of late the board has taken on a renewed commitment to developing a relationship with the members that honors their moral ownership role.

As we saw in chapter seven, the camp has evolved in its understanding of stewardship through all four stages of maturity. At first it was mere survival—getting kids to camp and successfully running a week's program without a major glitch was the best stewardship that the director and staff could muster.

But as the organization grew with fresh new directors bringing greater and greater experience to bear, stewardship grew through the stages of sustainability, growth and optimization. With each maturing, members and the stakeholders responded with increased support and enthusiasm. Five generations of families now count the camp as *their* camp, and support in donations, volunteer hours and passion makes the relationship between stakeholder and steward almost a dream come true. Recently the camp raised over a million dollars from its members, constituent families and supporters for a major capital improvement campaign while donations increased to the general operating fund at the same time! The camp operates with only seven full-time staff members with all other duties performed by unpaid volunteers. Volunteers have to sign up to work at camp as far in advance as possible since waiting lists start forming long before summer season even begins. The youth see working as a volunteer as one of the most important leadership development opportunities available to them, and their supporting churches view camp as a critical part of their evangelistic and leadership training programs. Rental groups have to book their weekend retreat years in advance in order to get a spot. And all of this occurs on a mere sixteen acres of land—which the camp doesn't own—and a 125-bed capacity.

An important part of this stewardship success story is the reality of how long it has taken to get to this point: fifty-five years. Nothing changed overnight, and each struggle with new stewardship responsibilities came with considerable conversation, some pushback and the occasional setback. Several board members have personally lived and wrestled through almost every major stage of the camp's maturation since they have served for more than thirty-five years, breaking every assumption about board "best practices." The current executive director has been either a volunteer or a staff member for more than forty years now. That longevity in the staff, board, constituents and stakeholders has played a key role in the organization's stewardship maturity. So it doesn't take a huge organization, lots of money, or best-in-class consultants to lead a group of leaders and an organization into true steward leadership. It takes patience and persistence.

We end with a call to apply the steward leadership model outside the nonprofit sector. Experts estimate that there are approximately 28 million businesses in the United States, from sole proprietorships to the self-employed to the nation's largest employers. These businesses employ a labor force of approximately 155 million people. Using simplistic math and some broad assumptions, that means that for every person considered a "business owner," there are at least five other people who are employed by those businesses and are not owners. In publicly traded companies, owners are clearly defined as stockholders, and everyone who works in the company does so as stewards of the stockholders. When we look outside the labor force to education, civil service, politics and the military, we can safely say that nearly all people who work in these sectors are stewards of resources they do not own.

Therefore, the vast majority of workers in the United States are stewards who are managing and using resources they do not personally own. They need to understand their stewardship role, and the leaders within these sectors need to learn how to lead as steward leaders. I believe this even includes owners of for-profit businesses, who in God's economy are stewards just as much as their employees.

At the beginning of this book I shared with you my belief: that steward leadership has the potential to change the face of nonprofit leadership forever. I believe the same is also true for every other sector of life where leadership is expressed. Since the concept is still young, more research needs to be done to more fully develop steward leadership as a model. And specialists in each sector of work life need to lend their understanding to the unique application of steward leadership to their sector. Consider the following comments as a beginning:

Steward leadership among professional managers. Many large companies have absentee owners who have placed control of the company in the hands of professional leaders and managers. These people are the true embodiment of steward leaders who manage resources belonging to a known owner or owners. Most are aware of their non-ownership role, but they may never have been given the language of steward leadership to focus their identity and responsibilities.

Steward leadership among publicly traded companies. Stockholders of publicly traded companies constitute a pool of owners whose input to the managers is dictated by rules, stockholder votes and bylaws. Similar to nonprofit stakeholders, stockholders rarely speak with one voice, but the policies surrounding stockholder meetings and input are generally defined.

Why then has there been a spate of bad publicity surrounding the abusive actions of public company leaders? I would venture to suggest that the vast majority of these failures of leadership are failures of stewardship. The lure of money through acting like an owner may be too great, and the only solution that I see is for these leaders to be selected based as much on their character and stewardship attitudes as on their business expertise.

Steward leadership in education. Most people I know in education have a high respect for the public trust they are given to educate our children and future members of the workforce. Many have never heard of steward leadership or have limited views of stewardship. School boards and academic committees present a unique challenge to governance and stewardship, but those who best understand their stewardship role can apply the tenets of steward leadership to these important community roles.

Steward leadership in the military. The military seems to be one place where all recruits are indoctrinated into their role as servants of the nation, so this is one sector where the language and concepts of stewardship and steward leadership should be able to find quick adoption. But as in education, it will take the work of those who know this sector to best translate the concepts into language and images that are appropriate.

Steward leadership in civil service and politics. People in civil service share many of the altruistic characteristics of nonprofit employees. They know they are there to serve the citizenry and all the resources at their disposal belong to the community at large. So why are there higher levels of dissatisfaction with their performance than in the nonprofit sector? Is there a failure of understanding concerning the significant stewardship role they play for the benefit of the rest of us? Who wouldn't stand up and cheer a politician who came out unambiguously and continuously with the identity and character of "a steward of the people"?

Steward leadership among business owners. As we previously discussed, in God's economy there is no one who is not a steward, which includes those who in the human realm actually own the businesses of today. You will find some business owners who act with an owner's mindset, assuming that they can make decisions based purely on their own needs and desires and are not accountable to anyone else. But I have found in the executive coaching work I do, most have a steward's attitude toward the business resources that they own, even if they are not believers. They believe that their business exists for more than just their own benefit and that good stewardship is a strength to good business. Business owners do need help, however, in knowing how to fully express their stewardship responsibilities and how to be accountable to God and their community for the resources under their management.

Steward leadership in the family. We would be deficient if we didn't conclude with one of the largest groups of people—husbands and wives, mothers and fathers—who have the privilege of living like stewards every day as they manage their families and households. Scripture clearly demonstrates through the Proverbs 31 woman and many other passages how important family stewardship is since good stewardship not only preserves and grows family resources, it recognizes that even our children are a gift from God on loan to us for a season. The Proverbs 31 woman is a steward leader is every sense of the word as she not only influences her own household through her stewardship but also impacts her community. We have also seen how the historical origin of the steward as the *oikonomos* or household manager was considered a core role and responsibility in society. Homemakers, stay-at-home moms and parents can be as much steward leaders as well-known business executives in their community.

Steward leaders. They served at the center of society for thousands of years and can be in even greater positions of influence today because of the growth in opportunity that individual citizens experience. Imagine what society would be like if we were surrounded by steward leaders and individual stewards at every level and in every sector?

Acknowledgments

It was almost twenty-five years after I graduated with a master's degree that I came up with the harebrained idea of going back to school to get my PhD. Not only was I going back to academia in my mid-fifties, but I wanted to study abroad in Scotland. Debbie, my wife of forty years, was the first to encourage me to do it, even though we still had kids at home and I planned on continuing to run a large publishing company during my studies. Debbie tops my list of those I want to acknowledge and thank for believing in my dream and passion to study a subject I had been mulling over for years.

The next person who deserves a great deal of thanks is Dr. David Molyneaux, my original sponsoring professor at the University of Aberdeen in Scotland. He paved the way for an older student like me to fit PhD studies into a busy lifestyle. He advocated to the university to shorten the residency requirement and eliminate many of the required classroom courses that were not necessary given my experience. But most of all, David responded to an unsolicited email from someone he had never met who had a dream to develop this new model called steward leadership. He loved the idea. He continuously introduced me to ideas, books and professors until his untimely death in the middle of my studies. My path was set, and God had other work for him in heaven.

When I started these studies, I thought I was on my own since little had been written about steward leadership. But I slowly came to know people here and there who were thinking similar thoughts, and we began to band together into a steward leader community. The first to lend his support and growing knowledge of the field was Dr. Scott Rodin, who had been writing on stewardship and the steward leader for some time. The two of us bonded quickly and soon found ourselves developing the Steward Leader Initiative, a collective that brings together others who are researching, writing and speaking on the steward and steward leadership. Early collaborators who joined in this community included Dr. Gary Hoag, Wes Willmer, Brett Elder and Mark Vincent. We presented papers to one another, listened to criticism and constructive comments, and developed our ideas further as a result. Many others have since joined our community as we continue to meet at least annually to be "iron sharpening iron."

The nonprofit community in my hometown of Colorado Springs and beyond has strongly embraced steward leadership and has contributed to its development. All of you who anonymously participated in my original research were of tremendous help with your time and clarity. Jon Hirst, Kurt Wilson, Bob Fryling, James Ferrier, Marybeth Leavell, Peter Carino, Calvin VanHeukelem and Mike Johnson each gave me constructive and critical comments about an earlier version of the manuscript and helped me make necessary strategic decisions in my writing.

I especially want to thank those far and wide who have been working tirelessly as nonprofit executive directors and board members: your encouragement, ideas and participation in contributing many real-life stories are scattered throughout this book and give it a "lived-in" feel. You also know who you are: Howard Brooks, Dirk Ailts, Brian Simmons, Dan Faulkner, Laura McGuire, Howard Rich, Kip Warton and many more who encouraged me. It took a community to write this book.

Notes

1 The Distinct Challenges of Nonprofit Organizational Leadership

[1]Peter F. Drucker, *Managing the Nonprofit Organization: Principles and Practices* (New York: Harper Business, 1990), xiv.

[2]Dennis R. Young, "Executive Leadership in Nonprofit Organizations," in *The Nonprofit Sector: A Research Handbook*, ed. Walter Powell (New Haven, CT: Yale University Press, 1987), 167-79.

[3]Rob Paton and Chris Cornforth, "What's Different About Managing in Voluntary and Non-Profit Organizations?," in *Issues in Voluntary and Non-Profit Management*, ed. Julian Batsleer, Chris Cornforth and Rob Paton (Workingham, MA: Addison-Wesley, 1992), 36-46.

[4]Robert D. Herman and Dick Heimovics, "Executive Leadership," in *The Jossey-Bass Handbook of Nonprofit Leadership and Management*, ed. Robert D. Herman (San Francisco: Jossey-Bass, 1994), 137-53.

[5]Burt Nanus and Steven Dobbs, *Leaders Who Make a Difference: Essential Strategies for Meeting the Nonprofit Challenge* (San Francisco: Jossey-Bass, 1999).

[6]Victor Sohmen, "A Leadership Model for Nonprofit Projects," in *Improving Leadership in Nonprofit Organizations*, ed. Ronald E. Riggio and Sarah Smith Orr (San Francisco: Jossey-Bass, 2004), 219-33.

[7]Jeanne Bell, Richard Moyers and Timothy Wolfred, *Daring to Lead 2006: A National Study of Nonprofit Executive Leadership* (San Francisco: CompassPoint and The Meyer Foundation, 2006), 3.

[8]Jeanne Peters, Timothy Wolfred and Michael Allison, *Daring to Lead: Nonprofit Executive Directors and Their Work Experience* (San Francisco: CompassPoint, 2001).

2 The Historical Steward of Classical Greco-Roman Culture

[1]A. H. M. Jones, "Slavery in the Ancient World," in *Slavery in Classical Antiquity: Views and Controversies*, ed. Moses I. Finley (New York: Barnes and Noble, 1968), 3.

[2]John Reumann, "The Use of Oikonomia and Related Terms in Greek Sources to About AD 100, as a Background for Patristic Applications" (PhD dissertation, University of Pennsylvania, 1957). More scholars as of late are agreeing with Reumann's etymology of *oikonomos*. Earlier researchers mistakenly assumed that *oikonomos* was derived from two nouns, *oikos* (*house*) and *nomos* (*law*).

[3]Francis Brown, S. R. Driver and Charles A. Briggs, *Hebrew and English Lexicon of the Old Testament* (Oxford: Clarendon Press, 1907), 254.

[4]W. E. Vine, *An Expository Dictionary of New Testament Words* (Old Tappan, NJ: Fleming H. Revell, 1940), 183.

[5]John Crook, *Law and Life of Rome* (Ithaca, NY: Cornell University Press, 1967), 187-88.

[6]Jones, "Slavery in the Ancient World," 2.

[7]Keith R. Bradley, *Slavery and Society at Rome* (Cambridge: Cambridge University Press, 1994), 75. *Digest* is a name given to a compendium or digest of Roman law compiled by order of the emperor Justinian I in the sixth century.

[8]Xenophon, *Oeconomicus* 1.1-4.

[9]Sarah B. Pomeroy, *Oeconomicus: A Social and Historical Commentary* by Xenophon, trans. Sarah B. Pomeroy (Oxford: Clarendon Press, 1994), 217.

[10]Ibid.

[11]Marcus Porcius Cato and Marcus Terentius Varro, *On Agriculture*, trans. William D. Hooper, rev. Harrison B. Ash (Cambridge, MA: Harvard University Press, 1934), 1.18.

[12]William Linn Westermann, *The Slave Systems of Greek and Roman Antiquity* (Philadelphia: American Philosophical Society, 1955), 20.

[13]Ibid., 26.

[14]William Thalmann, interview by the author, February 22, 2007, Los Angeles.

[15]Jones, "Slavery in the Ancient World," 1.

[16]Lucius Junius Moderatus Columella, *On Agriculture*, trans. Harrison B. Ash (Cambridge, MA: Harvard University Press, 1968), 11.1.3.

[17]Cato, *On Agriculture* 5.5.

[18]Columella, *On Agriculture* 1.7.13-14.

[19]Ibid., 11.1.14.

[20]Ibid., 1.8.5.

[21]Ibid., 11.1.5-7.

[22]Ibid., 11.1.7.

[23]Ibid., 11.1.4.

[24]Xenophon, *Oeconomicus* 12.6-12.

[25]Cato, *On Agriculture* 5.2.

[26]Columella, *On Agriculture* 11.1.5.

[27]Marcus Porcius Cato, *Cato on Farming: De Agricultura*, trans. Andrew Dalby (Blackawton, UK: Prospect Books, 1998), 65.

[28]Cato, *On Agriculture* 2.1-7.

[29]Ibid., 5.4.

[30]Columella, *On Agriculture* 11.1.24.

[31]Ibid., 11.1.23.

[32]Ibid., 11.1.18-19.

[33]Ibid., 1.8.5.

[34]Ibid., 11.1.18.

[35]Ibid., 11.1.6.

[36]Ibid., 1.8.10.

[37]Ibid., 11.1.20.

[38]Cato, *On Agriculture* 5.4.

[39]Columella, *On Agriculture* 12.1.5.

[40]Ibid., 11.1.17.

[41]Cato, *On Agriculture* 5.2.

[42]Columella, *On Agriculture* 11.1.25.

[43]Xenophon, *Oeconomicus* 21.9.

[44]Columella, *On Agriculture* 11.1.7-8.

[45]Xenophon, *Oeconomicus* 16.14.

[46]Varro, *On Agriculture* 1.16.

[47]Warren Bennis and Burt Nanus, *Leaders: The Strategies for Taking Charge* (New York: Harper, 1985), 204.

[48]Columella, *On Agriculture* 11.1.13-14.

[49]Xenophon, *Oeconomicus* 7.4.

[50]Bob Biehl, "Quick Wisdom Email," May 9, 2007, www.quickwisdom.com/Quick WisdomEmails/101110/Failure.lsp.

[51]Peter Block, *Stewardship: Choosing Service over Self-Interest* (San Francisco: Berrett-Koehler, 1993), 41-51.

[52]Larry C. Spears, *Insights on Leadership: Service, Stewardship, Spirit, and Servant-Leadership* (New York: John Wiley and Sons, 1998), 85.

[53]Columella, *On Agriculture* 11.1.4.

[54]Richard Ayres, "Leading by Example: How We Learn About Leadership," paper presented at the National Executive Institute Associates June 2004 Annual Conference, Sun Valley, Idaho, June 9-13, 2004, www.neiassociates.org/leadingbyexample.

[55]Cynthia Berryman-Fink and Charles Fink, *The Manager's Desk Reference*, 2nd ed. (New York: AMACOM, 1996), 167.

[56]Columella, *On Agriculture* 11.19.

[57]James M. Kouzes and Barry Z. Posner, *The Leadership Challenge*, 3rd ed. (San Francisco: Jossey-Bass, 2002), 281.

3 THE HISTORICAL STEWARD OF THE BIBLE

[1]An equally profitable word analysis could also be conducted in the Septuagint (LXX)—the Koine Greek version of the Old Testament translated between the

third and first century BC—but I have given priority to the Hebrew text to limit the scope of this book.

[2]David L. Gersch, "A Study of the Term *Ho Oikonomos*: Its Semantic Development and Its Meaning in the New Testament" (master's thesis, St. Paul Seminary, 1974), 18.

[3]Ibid., 23.

[4]Helge Brattgard, *God's Stewards: A Theological Study of the Principles and Practices of Stewardship*, trans. Gene J. Lund (Minneapolis: Augsburg, 1963), 41.

[5]Ibid.

[6]Douglas John Hall, *The Steward: A Biblical Symbol Come of Age* (Grand Rapids: Eerdmans, 1990), 33.

[7]Robert R. Ellis, "Divine Gift and Human Response: An Old Testament Model of Stewardship," *Southwestern Journal of Theology* 32, no. 2 (1995): 5.

[8]Ben Gill, *Stewardship: The Biblical Basis for Living* (Arlington, TX: The Summit Publishing Group, 1996), 17.

[9]Richard K. Taylor, *Economics and the Gospel* (Philadelphia: United Church Press, 1973), 25.

[10]The synoptic parallel for Luke's use of *oikonomos* is found in Mt 24:45, which uses the word *doulos*, the most common word in Greek for "slave" or "servant." In Luke's version of the same parable, he later switches to the same common term *doulos* (repeated four times in Lk 12:43-47) and does not repeat the more concrete *oikonomos*. However, this does not negate the specific application of *oikonomos* as evidenced by its forward placement. It does support the fact that most first-century stewards were still slaves.

[11]R. Scott Rodin, *Stewards in the Kingdom: A Theology of Life in All Its Fullness* (Downers Grove, IL: InterVarsity Press, 2000), 29-30.

[12]*logon*: The word generally means "speech, word" or by usage "written words or speeches," and then by application to the world of commerce, "make an accounting." Munro and Mouritsen add more detail concerning the classical method of stewardship accounting: "Under such systems, down through the eighteenth century, the dominant form of operative power relation was that of stewardship, and the form of one's responsibility was to be answerable after the fact and grosso modo. So, for instance, on ancient and medieval estates, the steward (or bailiff or reeve) would be called every so often to account (perhaps annually, perhaps more sporadically), and made to answer for the detail of their stewardship. There would typically be some inspection of receipts and payments of money and produce, a form of information which is already found on estates in Greco-Roman antiquity (Macve, 1985). There might be an elaborate formal ritual, as in the medieval audit, the solemn and detailed hearing and examining of these accounts." Rolland Munro and Jan Mouritsen, eds., *Accountability: Power, Ethos, and the Technologies of Managing* (London: International Thomson Business Press, 1996), 275.

[13]R. C. H. Lenski, *The Interpretation of St. Luke's Gospel* (Minneapolis: Augsburg, 1946), 834.

[14]An interesting debate that is gaining ground in some circles is the question whether endowments, a common practice of many educational and larger nonprofit organizations, is wise stewardship or a violation of the stewardship principle of "working" assets. Time does not allow that debate to be argued in this book but it is a worthwhile stewardship question.

[15]Randy Alcorn, *Money, Possessions, and Eternity*, rev. ed. (Wheaton, IL: Tyndale House, 2003), 149.

[16]Rodin, *Stewards in the Kingdom*, 30.

[17]Ibid., 29-30.

[18]Ibid., 116.

[19]Peter Block, *Stewardship: Choosing Service over Self-Interest* (San Francisco: Berrett-Koehler, 1993), 41.

4 THE STEWARD LEADERSHIP MODEL

[1]Max De Pree, *Leadership Is an Art* (New York: Bantam Doubleday Dell, 1989), 12-13.

[2]Peter M. Senge, *The Fifth Discipline: The Art and Practice of the Learning Organization* (New York: Doubleday/Currency, 1990), 346.

[3]J. Robert Clinton, *Leadership Emergence Theory: A Self-Study Manual for Analyzing the Development of a Christian Leader* (Altadena, CA: Barnabas Resources, 1989), 57.

[4]Ibid., 58.

[5]David Birkenstock, "Leadership: The Key Dimension in Adventist Tertiary Educational Administration," paper prepared for the International Faith and Learning Seminar, 1993, www.aiias.edu/ict/vol_12/12cc_037-048.htm.

[6]Peter Block, *Stewardship: Choosing Service over Self-Interest* (San Francisco: Berrett-Koehler, 1993), xx.

[7]Ibid., 18.

[8]Richard Higginson, *Transforming Leadership: A Christian Approach to Management* (London: SPCK, 1996), 50.

[9]Richard L. Daft, *Leadership: Theory and Practice* (Fort Worth: Dryden Press, 1999), 371.

[10]Peter C. Brinckerhoff, *Nonprofit Stewardship: A Better Way to Lead Your Mission-Based Organization* (St. Paul, MN: Amherst H. Wilder Foundation, 2004), 3-4.

[11]Ibid., 66.

[12]Ibid., 6.

[13]R. Scott Rodin, *The Steward Leader: Transforming People, Organizations and Communities* (Downers Grove, IL: InterVarsity Press, 2010), 8.

[14]Ibid., 21.

[15]John Carver, *The Policy Governance Model and the Role of the Board Member* (San Francisco: Jossey-Bass, 2009).

[16]Lex Donaldson, "The Ethereal Hand: Organizational Economics and Management Theory," *Academy of Management Review* 15, no. 3 (1990): 369-81.

[17]Rodin in *The Steward Leader* offers many helpful comparisons between the steward leader and the owner leader.

[18]In proposing this chain of accountability, I acknowledge the contribution of Raymond Kao, Kenneth Kao and Rowland Kao, *An Entrepreneurial Approach to Stewardship Accountability: Corporate Residual and Global Poverty* (Singapore: World Scientific, 2005), who offer a form of accountability that they call the "hierarchy of stewardship responsibility" (140-41) and the "stewardship proprietary decision-making hierarchy" (62).

5 The Steward Leader

[1]I define "distinctive characteristics" as those rooted in the distinct behaviors and responsibilities of stewardship or are rarely or only occasionally identified by other trait approaches to leadership. It is not that these steward leader characteristics are never found in other models. Rather, they are generally not emphasized by others or they have distinctive expressions in the context of steward leadership.

[2]Peter G. Northouse, *Leadership: Theory and Practice*, 4th ed. (Thousand Oaks, CA: Sage Publications, 2007), 3.

[3]Warren Bennis and Burt Nanus, *Leaders: The Strategies for Taking Charge* (New York: Harper, 1985), 21.

[4]Joseph C. Rost, *Leadership for the Twenty-First Century* (Westport, CT: Praeger Publishers, 1991).

[5]Douglas McGregor, *The Human Side of Enterprise* (New York: McGraw, 1960).

[6]Northouse, *Leadership*, 2-3.

[7]Robert K. Greenleaf, *The Servant as Leader* (Indianapolis: Robert K. Greenleaf Center for Servant-Leadership, 1970), 7.

6 How Steward Leadership Compares to Servant Leadership

[1]Robert K. Greenleaf, *The Servant as Leader* (Indianapolis: Robert K. Greenleaf Center for Servant-Leadership, 1970), 7.

[2]Max De Pree, *Leadership Is an Art* (New York: Bantam Doubleday Dell, 1989), 12.

[3]Larry C. Spears, ed., *Reflections on Leadership: How Robert K. Greenleaf's Theory of Servant-Leadership Influenced Today's Top Management Thinkers* (New York: John Wiley and Sons, 1995), 4-7.

[4]Jane Fryar, *Servant Leadership: Setting Leaders Free* (St. Louis: Concordia Publishing House, 2001), 11.

[5]Ibid., 12.

[6]Ken Blanchard and Phil Hodges, *Servant Leader: Transforming Your Heart, Head, Hands and Habits* (Nashville: J. Countryman Books, 2002).

[7]Eugene Peterson, "Follow the Leader," *Fuller Focus*, Fall 2001, 31.

[8]Nicholas A. Beadles II, "Stewardship-Leadership: A Biblical Refinement of Servant-Leadership," *Journal of Biblical Integration*, Fall 2000, 30.

7 Stages in the Development of Stewardship

[1]A. C. Littleton, *Accounting Evolution to 1900* (New York: American Institute Publishing Co., 1933), 264.

[2]Andrew Higson and Mike Tayles, "A Reconsideration of the Nature of Stewardship," *Journal of Applied Research* 4, no. 2 (1998): 71.

[3]Littleton, *Accounting Evolution,* 126.

[4]Jacob Birnberg, "The Role of Accounting in Financial Disclosure," *Accounting, Organizations and Society* 5, no. 1 (1980): 73.

[5]Ibid.

[6]Thomas H. Jeavons, *When the Bottom Line Is Faithfulness: Management of Christian Service Organizations* (Bloomington: Indiana University Press, 1994), 76.

[7]According to Drucker, most nonprofit organizations "are out to maximize rather than optimize. 'Our mission will not be completed,' asserts the head of the Crusade Against Hunger, 'as long as there is one child on the earth going to bed hungry.' . . . If the goal is maximization, it can never be attained. Indeed, the closer one comes toward attaining one's objective, the more efforts are called for. For, once optimization has been reached (and the optimum in most efforts lies between 75 and 80 percent of theoretical maximum), additional costs go up exponentially while additional results fall off exponentially. The closer a public-service institution comes to attaining its objectives, the more frustrated it will be and the harder it will work on what it is already doing." Peter F. Drucker, *Innovation and Entrepreneurship* (New York: Harper & Row, 1985), 180.

8 Steward Leadership in the Nonprofit Organization

[1]Peter D. Hall, "Historical Perspectives on Nonprofit Organizations in the United States," in *The Jossey-Bass Handbook of Nonprofit Leadership and Management*, ed. Robert D. Herman (San Francisco: Jossey-Bass, 1994), 5.

[2]Peter F. Drucker, *The New Realities: In Government and Politics, in Economics and Business, in Society and World View* (New York: Harper Collins, 1989), 204.

[3]Lester M. Salamon, *The State of Nonprofit America* (Washington, DC: Brookings Institution Press, 2002), 6-7.

[4]Peter F. Drucker, *Managing the Non-Profit Organization: Principles and Practices* (New York: Harper Business, 1990).

9 The Nonprofit Board as Steward Leader

[1]Midwest Center for Nonprofit Leadership, "The Legal Duties of the Nonprofit Board and Its Members" (University of Missouri Kansas City, 2010), 1; bloch.umkc.edu/mwcnl/resources/documents/legal-duties.pdf.

[2]Ibid.

[3]*Fiduciary* fundamentally means "a trust of property or power to a person for the benefit of another," which is a similar definition as stewardship.

[4]Michael Batts, *Board Member Orientation* (Orlando: Accountability Press, 2011).

[5]Ruth McCambridge, "Understanding the Power of Nonprofit Governance," *Nonprofit and Voluntary Sector Quarterly* 33, no. 2 (June 2004): 351.

[6]John Carver, *Boards That Make a Difference: A New Design for Leadership in Nonprofit and Public Organizations* (San Francisco: Jossey-Bass, 2006).

10 THE CEO/EXECUTIVE DIRECTOR AS STEWARD LEADER

[1]Howard Rich, personal letter to the author, July 3, 2015.

[2]John Carver, *Boards That Make a Difference: A New Design for Leadership in Nonprofit and Public Organizations* (San Francisco: Jossey-Bass, 2006).

[3]Robert D. Herman and Dick Heimovics, "Executive Leadership," in *The Jossey-Bass Handbook of Nonprofit Leadership and Management*, ed. Robert D. Herman (San Francisco: Jossey-Bass, 1994).

[4]Ibid., 141.

[5]Ibid.

[6]I took an earlier version of a chart on board governance proposed by Richard Chait, William Ryan and Barbara Taylor, *Governance as Leadership: Reframing the Work of Nonprofit Boards* (Hoboken, NJ: John Wiley & Sons, 2004), 98, and modified it.

[7]Burt Nanus and Steven Dobbs, *Leaders Who Make a Difference: Essential Strategies for Meeting the Nonprofit Challenge* (San Francisco: Jossey-Bass, 1999), 11-12.

[8]Peter F. Drucker, *Innovation and Entrepreneurship* (New York: Harper & Row, 1985).

[9]Dennis R. Young, "Executive Leadership in Nonprofit Organizations," *The Nonprofit Sector: A Research Handbook*, ed. Walter Powell (New Haven, CT: Yale University Press, 1987), 172.

[10]Matthew Elliott, personal letter to the author, August 10, 2015.

11 THE NONPROFIT STAFF AS STEWARDS

[1]Peter F. Drucker, *Innovation and Entrepreneurship* (New York: Harper & Row, 1985), 180.

About the Author

Kent Wilson was born and raised in Colorado and currently resides in Colorado Springs. He attended Stanford University where he received a BS in electrical engineering design and a BA in psychology. He also has a master of divinity from Denver Seminary. In his last year of college Kent married Deborah, to whom he has been married for more than forty years. They have three children and seven grandchildren.

Kent completed his PhD studies at the University of Aberdeen in Scotland after conducting research in the area of steward leadership for nonprofit organizations. He lectures widely on steward leadership, stewardship and nonprofit leadership. He is also the author of three books on publishing and numerous magazine and journal articles on leadership, business management, steward leadership and personal spiritual growth.

Currently Kent is an executive coach and chair for Vistage International, an international CEO development organization. As an executive coach he brings people who run businesses into small peer-advisory groups and coaches them in leadership, business management and life skills. He is also the executive director of the Nonprofit Leadership Exchange (NLE), his own leader development and consulting organization that serves nonprofit CEOs in the same way. Recently he created and directs the national Leader2Leader peer advisory program for nonprofit CEOs under the Christian Leadership Alliance.

Kent serves as president and chairman of the Wilson Foundation started by his grandfather. It is an operating foundation (does not accept grant requests) that supports the development of Christian literature for third-world Christians. He has worked most of his adult life in a variety of nonprofit organizations, from the church pastorate to children's camping ministry to a commercial nonprofit Christian publishing company. He sits on the board of multiple nonprofit organizations, often in the role as chairman. His interest in steward leadership led Kent to partner with Dr. Scott Rodin to establish the Steward Leader Institute, which coordinates scholarship, dialogue and publishing in steward leadership.

You can contact Dr. Kent Wilson about speaking on steward leadership, helping your board develop as steward leaders or consulting with your organization:

Dr. Kent R. Wilson
Email: kent@nlegroups.org
Phone: 719-339-9935

Subject Index

Scripture Index